QUAINT CORNERS
OF
ANCIENT EMPIRES

QUAINT CORNERS
OF
ANCIENT EMPIRES

SOUTHERN INDIA, BURMA,
AND
MANILA

MICHAEL MYERS SHOEMAKER

GYAN

Published by

GYAN

Gyan Publishing House
5, Ansari Road
Daryaganj, New Delhi-110002
Phone: 011-47034999, 9811692060
E-mail: books@gyanbooks.com

Distribution Network
gyanbooks.com
India, USA, Canada, UK, Australia

ISBN: 978-93-7169-351-6 (PB)

First Published, 1899

2nd Impression 2025

Printed at: Gyan Press, Delhi.

QUAINT CORNERS OF ANCIENT EMPIRES
Author: MICHAEL MYERS SHOEMAKER

SANTA LUCIA GATE, MONASTERY OF AUGUSTINES, MANILA.

(Frontispiece.)

QUAINT CORNERS
OF
ANCIENT EMPIRES

SOUTHERN INDIA, BURMA
AND
MANILA

BY

MICHAEL MEYERS SHOEMAKER

Author of "Islands of the Southern Seas," and "Palaces and Prisons of Mary Queen of Scots"

Illustrated

1899

TO MY NEPHEW

LIEUTENANT ISRAEL PUTNAM

UNITED STATES ARMY

WHO RECEIVED HIS BAPTISM OF FIRE

AT SAN JUAN DEL MONTE, MANILA

ON HIS TWENTY-FIRST BIRTHDAY

PREFACE

"OF making many books there is no end" may already be said concerning this Spanish-American war, but, so far, no apology is needed for presenting to our public any work upon the Philippines. If an increase of the army is demanded for these islands it will not be long before every State in the Union will have men there in whom they are directly interested, and the theatre in which those soldiers must play their parts, and perhaps end their lives, cannot but be of interest to those left behind them, especially to their wives, mothers, and sisters. Therefore I venture to think that the following account of the city of Manila with its surroundings will prove acceptable. If it helps "the women who wait," and who in so doing fight the hardest of all battles, to tide over any of the weary hours, it will have more than accomplished its purpose.

I have told the story of the friars in the Philippines as I learned it from the highest English and American authorities in Manila,—all men who have lived there for years,—as I have read it in that standard work of Foreman's, *The Philippine Islands*, and also as the *official records* give it. It has not been pleasant writing, and it may be claimed that no good can come from its publication. Granted, so long as the archipelago belonged to another nation; but the United States are now responsible for what goes on in those islands, and certainly if the actions of these friars are condoned, if silence is allowed to drop its mantle upon them, they will take heart and continue in their old lines—they have never known any other—with the conclusion on the part of the people that the Americans are no better or wiser than the Spaniards, and that one bad master has been exchanged for another. Instead thereof, they must be convinced that our courts and laws are for the protection of both friars and people, and that justice and just punishment will be meted out to both. I do not consider that these friars have anything in common with the enlightened Catholics of Europe and America. They are of the Dark Ages, and the account of their actions will thoroughly astonish the members of that great Church in other lands—actions so terrible that they have completely wiped from the memory of the natives all recollections of any good they (the friars) may have accomplished, driving the people into taking vengeance even upon the churches and the graves of the dead. These friars are the power with which we shall have the greatest struggle, because they have the most to lose through an enlightened form of government, and this struggle will be all the more deadly because they will work in secret, attack in the dark. Have we a Dictator Diaz to send out there? Surely, when the American people, both Catholic and Protestant, especially the former, thoroughly understand the matter, they will arise and, taking arms against this sea of troubles, end them, both in the Philippines and in Porto Rico, from whence, I am told, like reports have come. Then the daily press will no longer be "afraid to publish," as the editor of a great American journal told me is now the case, facts about any occurrences in the lands over which waves our national banner.

But before reading the chapters on Manila we will journey through Southern India, from Ceylon to the grandest and least known of all Hindoo temples—"Rameswaram" on Adam's Bridge. Thence to fantastic Madura and stately Tanjore. Then passing via Madras and the Bay of Bengal we will land at Rangoon under that dazzling shrine of the Buddhists, the Great Pagoda. We will sail up the Irrawaddy for a thousand miles, almost reaching China; and, returning, we will pause in Mandalay, and, taking quarters in the palace of the Queen, inspect that romantic city with its dragon thrones, its golden palaces, monasteries, and countless pagodas, while we listen to its many legends of splendour founded upon wholesale slaughter. Passing with the gay throngs once more to the river, we will drift on to where the ancient city of Pagahn has stood silent and deserted for seven hundred years—Pagahn with its ten thousand shrines. What is Rome to this? Onward down the river we will pass to Prome, and from thence journey to Rangoon, where we will take ship for Manila.

M. M. S.

April, 1899.

CONTENTS

CHAPTER I

RAMESWARAM

CHAPTER II

THE PLAGUE

CHAPTER III

MADURA

CHAPTER IV

TANJORE

CHAPTER V

MADRAS

CHAPTER VI

BAY OF BENGAL

CHAPTER VII

BURMA

CHAPTER VIII

IRRAWADDY AND MANDALAY

CHAPTER IX

MONASTERIES

CHAPTER X

BURMESE CUSTOMS

CHAPTER XI

ANCIENT PAGAHN

CHAPTER XII

RANGOON

CHAPTER XIII

EN ROUTE TO MANILA

CHAPTER XVI

OLD MANILA

CHAPTER XVII

RAMBLES IN OLD MANILA

CHAPTER XVIII

THE FRIARS

ILLUSTRATIONS

MANILA

QUAINT CORNERS OF ANCIENT EMPIRES

CHAPTER I

RAMESWARAM

The Great Temple of Rameswaram—Its Isolated Position and the Way thither—Its Vast Corridors, Holy Tanks, Processions, Jewels, and Legends—Life on the Island of Paumben—Return to Colombo—Indian Magicians—Military Church Service.

RAMESWARAM, the most venerated, the most magnificent, and the largest of Hindoo temples, is situated on a lonely, sandy island close under the shores of Southern India, an island which, with its neighbours and the connecting reefs, forms what is called Adam's Bridge, uniting Ceylon with the continent of Asia. In the narrow passages open to the sea, the waters make constant complaint against their tumultuous existence. During the south-west monsoon the waves of the Indian Ocean are driven northward past Cape Comorin and on into the Gulf of Kandy (also called " Manar "), to be forced finally with tremendous roaring through these straits. When the monsoon from the north-east comes on, the waters of the Bay of Bengal are sent with equal power southward, so that here there is never any rest.

Holy Rameswaram, therefore, is not easy of access. The traveller to-day must take ship from Colombo or Nagapatam to Paumben, the seaport of this island. He will be landed from a native dhow on a rough coast. Those who carry him ashore will probably drop him just where the waves will reach to his knees. Paumben is a desolate collection of native huts, with the bungalows of two Englishmen who are stationed here as agents in the coolie trade to Ceylon. There is no Rest-house or Dak Bungalow, and unless the Englishmen take pity on you, you must sleep in the open air, inspected at frequent intervals by the many native dogs. I was so fortunate as to secure the good-will of Mr. Wilkinson, who turned over his bungalow to me, and placed at my disposal his gharry and bullocks. Climbing into the little black vehicle, I sat perforce with a foot out of each window, and was bowled along at a smart trot by the bullocks, after their driver had induced them to pass their stable.

Rameswaram is some eight miles distant across the island, and a comparatively good road has been constructed thereto by the Madras Government. The way is, as it were, an Indian Appian Way. There are many temples and shrines, many tanks and basins, wherein the people bathe and pray, while countless pilgrims pass onwards towards this Mecca of their faith. All the vivid colouring of

APPROACH TO RAMESWARAM.

the East, toned to an artistic softness, glows in the garments of the multitude. Moss green, dull red, and gold are the favoured hues; the material is coarse and cheap, but arranged with a grace never found in our world of fashion. Yonder dark-eyed maiden stands robed in scarlet; on each toe glitter two or three silver rings; her arms are laden with bangles almost to the elbows, and her ears bear long gold rings, while her left nostril has been pierced and a tiny gold flower shines against the dark skin. Yonder boy, clothed in a string around his loins, has eight rings piercing the rims of each of his ears. In the background rise the grotesque columns of a Hindoo shrine; its black, stone bull is covered with yellow flowers, while the roof of its pagoda holds countless images of Brahma in all his many shapes and attributes.

Here is a temple in the midst of a square basin full of slime. Down the steps which enclose it crowd the people, stooping ever and anon to question the many priests, and then bathing in and drinking the sacred water.

At last, at the end of the long avenue, rises the great gopura of the temple of Rameswaram, each receding story of which is encrusted with countless statues of Hindoo deities, which gaze down in indignant amazement at the solitary traveller in strange clothes, who comes in simple curiosity, and not as a pilgrim laden with gifts to the gods.

Passing through the portal which is formed by three monoliths, those at the sides being each nineteen feet in height, the traveller stands in silent wonder at the scene before him. A shadowy corridor stretches away until in the far perspective it ends in the sanctuary where a golden bull is all ablaze in the light of the noonday sun. The walls rise some thirty feet above one and are richly painted in Hindoo designs; each column is formed by the grotesque and colossal statue of some god or animal sacred to that creed, and is carved from a single stone. Here is the triple-faced god Brahma, yonder a grotesque ape, followed by a line of old maharajas. There is Shiva alone, and yonder the monkey-faced god Hanuman.

This great passage is but an entrance-hall, the first transverse corridor being some seven hundred feet long, but everywhere are to be seen the same flat roof, the same endless rows of grotesque columns, the same gorgeous yet subdued colouring. Through the openings on either side are, on the one hand, a sacred tank, on the other, several small sanctuaries.

Passing down this corridor, the traveller will enter one or the other of the great lateral halls of the temple, and here the true magnificence of Rameswaram is discovered. For this corridor, though of the same design and ornament as those already mentioned, is one thousand feet long. Its perspective is something marvellous. The glance of the beholder passes on and on until wearied with the journey to the farther end, which is almost lost in the shadowy distance. This corridor is three hundred feet longer than the Cathedral of St. Peter's. In fact, all the shrines of the world shrink into insignificance as one stands gazing down the vast spaces of Rameswaram.

For a more perfect comprehension, Rameswaram

may be described as a parallelogram; its side corridors are each one thousand feet long, the front and rear being each seven hundred and fifty, while the entrance corridors, piercing those of the front and rear in the centre and at right angles, are at least four hundred feet in length, and terminate in two sanctuaries. All of these corridors are of the same style and description, all of the same grotesque splendour.

Strangers are not allowed to approach the sanctuaries, but it is easily seen that they contain simply a stone or brazen bull, or a statue of some god, and that they are all very dirty. These vast temples contain no great central hall or chamber, merely these small shrines with the numerous corridors and open-air courts. Such a design is better adapted to the processions so dear to the heart of the Hindoo.

Seated in a shadowy nook I await the coming of the custodian of the treasury, having sent for him by one of the many attendants who continually flit hither and thither throughout all this vastness. Finally he comes—a fat, comfortable-looking Brahmin, arrayed in diaphanous white, with a white turban, his brown skin shining with its polishing of cocoanut oil. With almost courtly manners and in most excellent English he welcomes me and offers me a chair on the other side of a long table.

"You would see the jewels of the temple? They are under the charge of several keepers. I am but one of them. I cannot show you all. I will show you many. The treasures of Rameswaram have been estimated at fifteen lacs of rupees" (£6000 to the lac).

His attendants have in the meantime brought forth several ancient caskets, and the table is soon covered with bracelets, armlets, anklets, pendants, and crowns, all encrusted with stones of every known description, and evidently of great value, but like all Oriental work, the jewels are not well cut and do not show to advantage. They are used to decorate the gods, and also their attendants, when a procession is taking place. Rameswaram possesses an income of some $30,000 a year, and this Brahmin says that it is used up every year in paying for the processions, in feeding the poor, and paying the wages of the many hundreds of men in constant attendance upon the temple.

Everyone in the Hindoo world makes a pilgrimage, once at least, to this sacred spot, and the money left by the pilgrims counts up to many thousands and hundreds of thousands of dollars. It is said that the people living in the town are all wealthy, though there is certainly no evidence of it in clothing or dwellings.

My Brahmin, becoming garrulous as the shadows lengthen, wanders on into the legends of his temple:

"Vishnu became incarnate for the seventh time as the son of Dasaratha, the King of Ayoehya, for the purpose of destroying the giant demon Rávana, who was King of Lanka or Ceylon. Wandering in the forest of Dandaka—so says the Southern Indian tradition—Ráma lost his wife Sítá, who was carried off to Lanka by Rávana. Ráma pursued the ravisher, attended by the devotees, who assumed the shape of monkeys. Their general, Hanumán, made a bridge of rocks from India to Ceylon at Rámeshwaram, by which Ráma crossed, slew Rávana, and recovered his bride. But when he returned he was observed to have two shadows, a sign of sin of the deepest dye. This was because Rávana was of the race of Brahma, and Ráma took council with the divine sages to discover some means of expiating his crime. They advised him to build a temple and confine Shiva there in a lingam or phallus, which is the emblem of that deity. Ráma built the temple, and sent Hanumán to Kailása, the heaven of Shiva, to get a lingam. As he was a long time in returning, and the hour for dedicating the temple was approaching, Ráma induced his wife Sítá to model a phallus of the white sand of the seacoast. This she did, and Ráma set up the phallus thus moulded in the temple, which was forthwith dedicated to Shiva. Meantime, Hanumán returned with another phallus and was so angry at being forestalled that he endeavoured to pull up the other lingam, and broke his tail in the effort to twist it out. Hereupon Shiva and his consort appeared from the lingam, and said to Ráma, 'Whoever visits this lingam dedicated by thee, and bathes in the twenty-four sacred bathing-places, shall be free from sin and inherit heaven.' Then, to console Hanumán, Ráma placed the lingam he had brought on the north side of the one which had been already set up, and ordained that pilgrims should visit it first and then Ráma's lingam."

The narrator ceases as the shadows of the night are falling; the jewels gleam for an instant as they are taken away, and I depart after being decorated by the Brahmin with a garland of white flowers.

As we turn down the long southern corridor, its far end is illuminated by an approaching procession, and we stand aside to witness its passage. There are hundreds of white- and yellow-robed figures in the line; their faces are fantastically painted, while their eyes have a rapt, far-off expression. There are two triumphal cars, covered with lights and garlanded with flowers, the first bearing a brazen bull, the second a statue of Shiva. The jewels on both flash and glitter in the flare of countless torches.

It is said that human sacrifice sometimes occurs in Rameswaram, and one wonders whether it may not be going to occur now. This is idolatry pure and simple, and all things are possible to the devotees at these shrines. Be that as it may, we have no desire to follow the procession as it vanishes in the distance, but, on the contrary, a very distinct desire to get out into God's sunshine where these grotesque gods cannot mock and jeer at us as they seem to be doing now.

The trip to Rameswaram is not an easy one, especially at this time when there is great excitement about the plague, which is steadily creeping over the southern end of the peninsula. I have some difficulty in getting on board the ship to Colombo, even though I hold permission from the health authorities of that place to return there. It would have been an unpleasant and even serious matter to have been forced to disembark and remain on the island, but the ship finally moves on and the trouble is ended.

Sunshine and shadow chase each other closely through this life of ours. All nature smiles here to-

RAMESWARAM, ADAM'S BRIDGE.

day, yet across the brilliance of the sunlight passes a sad-faced woman with six children, the oldest not yet ten years of age. She is going home to England, having lost her husband in Madras. His pension ended with his life, and the poor woman has nothing but a return ticket for herself and family. What a sad face, and how justly so! The children, however, seem well cared for and are most considerate of the mother.

We have as passengers a Catholic bishop and four priests from Jafna, an important missionary post for all sects at the extreme northern end of Ceylon. The Catholic mission is the most prosperous, and I am told that this arises from two causes: first, because the ceremonials of that Church appeal more strongly to the Hindoo than do the simple services of the other denominations; and, second, because the Catholic priest comes out here for life. All his past and his people at home are buried from him forever. He enters among these people and lives their lives, adopting their modes in all ways. Hence he becomes one of them, and gets nearer to their inner lives than the missionaries of the other sects who carry home customs and manners with them, who live separate and apart from the people, who send their families to the hills and often go themselves on the first approach of hot weather. The world has rarely, if ever, heard of a Catholic priest deserting his post for any cause. I do not mean to state that our missionaries do so, but they certainly do not gain the hearts of these people as do the Romanists, and those who live here, and whose opportunities of judging are of course excellent, give the reasons as I have stated them. My information came from a member of the Church of England, an official who had lived in Ceylon for eighteen years, and whose work carried him to all sections of the island.

The gay harbour of Colombo is reached at last, and we pass ashore amidst the motley concourse which forever crowds these Eastern ports, pass upward into the cool shade of the Oriental Hotel and out upon its wide veranda, where one may find amusement at all times. Here are the merchants with precious stones, here are sellers of gold, and silverware, rare embroideries, and sandalwood—but watch those fakirs a while.

The statement has been made by such prestidigitateurs as Hermann and Heller that they have never seen any tricks by these men of India which they could not explain. Be that as it may, these common street magicians do some very clever things. Certainly the performance before the Grand Hotel Colombo this morning, under the blazing sunlight and not three feet from the looker-on, was remarkable. As to the mango-tree trick there appeared a strong resemblance between the tree grown yesterday and the one produced this morning. But it was in the other performances that the observers were most interested. In one instance, the fakir took a small jar of metal and handed it around to show that it was empty. Then placing a copper coin between his teeth he began to blow, and smoke soon issued from his mouth and nostrils; the jar, which was held aloft all the time, was found filled with water, which commenced to boil furiously. Casting it aside, he opened his mouth and ejected jets of living flame. Indeed the whole cavity of the throat appeared to be filled with fire which ignited anything with which it came in contact. We all saw the empty jar, the filled jar, the boiling water, and the fire, but the fire never approached the jar.

Another trick consisted in causing a dead and dried-up cobra to come to life—or so it appeared. The snake is usually kept in a small round flat basket with a closely fitting cover. This we saw was empty, and into it the fakir laid the flat dried skin of a dead serpent. Placing it not three feet from our circle, and in the brilliant light of the Southern sun, he covered the basket with its lid, and then made the usual passes with the inevitable cloth, about a yard square, which he held by two corners to show that it contained nothing. His costume consisted of one garment of the shirt order, the sleeves of which were tucked up at the shoulders, affording, it would seem, scant opportunity to hide anything; yet, when after a few waves of the cloth, he removed the lid of the basket, the dead snake was gone, and in its place rose the majestic hooded head and neck of one of the largest of cobras.

It must be remembered that when we see such work in England or America it is done at a distance, and on a stage, with all the assistance of stage lights and shadows, but in this case we were out in plain air, and near enough for the serpent to have stung us.

The last trick consisted in a display of apparently wonderful strength. A boy of ten years of age was tied up in a large scarf with its ends attached to two strong cords. At the ends of these cords were hollow brass cups about the size of an acorn. The fakir, raising the upper lid of each of his eyes, inserted these cups thereunder, and with the hollow side next to the eyeball, after which he pulled the eyelids well down. Then with hands on hips and head well back he arose to his full height, lifting the boy a foot and more off the ground and swinging him from side to side, the entire weight of course falling upon the brass cups. It seemed a marvel that the eyeballs were not destroyed. Perhaps those who understand these matters can explain all that was done, but certainly no magicians on our stages have accomplished similar feats, and yet these men are but common street performers.

But this is Sunday morning! let us desert the world of magic and attend the worship of the one true God. We have not far to go, as the church is just over yonder in the arcade, towards which all the English, civil and military, in Colombo are wending their way.

In Ceylon, the service of the Church of England is conducted upon strictly military principles. The parson's sermon this morning was short and sharp, and delivered with military precision. The lessons were read by an officer in uniform, and in such a tone as he would use in making a report to his superior, while the soldiers furnished the music. Several hundred of Great Britain's defenders were present, all in white duck uniforms touched with scarlet. In his box of state sat the Governor with his family and aides. Overhead waved the slowly swinging punkas, kept in motion by half a dozen disciples of Brahma, who, in common with some wise-looking monkeys in a tree outside, looked on in grave surprise at the simple worship of the Nazarene. The Hindoos were silent, but the monkeys chattered now and then as though questioning what it all meant, and upon the first sound of the trumpets fled away into the green gloom of the palms and the scarlet glory of the poincianas, through which the tropical sunlight filtered like drops of rain, rain perfumed by the spicy breezes wafting softly over the island and the slumbering Indian Ocean.

CHAPTER II

THE PLAGUE

The Plague—The Means whereby it Spreads—Immunity of Europeans—When the Rats Begin to Die—The Belief of the Natives as to its Origin—Opinion of the Bombay Doctors—The Towers of Silence during the Pest—The Gathering of the Vultures even from Turkestan.

IT is somewhat with fear and trembling that the traveller ventures into Southern India in these days of 1898,—not so much in fear of the plague as in dread of being quarantined in some impossible Indian village,—but if he is *en route* for Burma he must risk that, or waste three weeks in Ceylon waiting for a ship. So far this year, the pest has not broken out in the points to which we are going, Madura, Trichinopoly, Tanjore, and Madras, although there have been some few imported cases. It is, however, slowly creeping onward, and if it should enter Ceylon it would prove the total ruin of that island, as there would be no market for her tea.

The pest does not, as a rule, attack Europeans. How it is carried from point to point is as yet a mystery. It is not epidemic but contagious. Many think that the mosquitoes are the vehicle, others lay it to the rats, and there is a premium offered for every rat, dead or alive. Others believe that it is in the dust and mud and that the natives contract it through their feet. The wife of our Bombay consul suffered with it two years ago, and insists that she got it by inhaling the dust of the city. When one does succumb its work is short and sharp, and generally with one ending—death. Whole families have retired at night apparently in perfect health, and have been found dead in the morning. Two years ago the people fled from Bombay by tens of thousands, and the population decreased from four hundred thousand to seventy thousand. The hotels were closed because there were no servants to run them, and silence and solitude settled over the doomed city. To-day, though the place is still infected, the cases are comparatively few and the people have returned and pay no further attention to the dreaded disease.

"First-class" travellers do not suffer much inconvenience, save from frequent medical inspection, but there is no doubt that many of the native officials make the pest a cause for blackmail. Twenty rupees would cause any one of them to pass you onward, unless you were mortally stricken, in which case you would not care whether you passed or not.

In India the pest thrives in cold weather because the people then gather indoors in a wretched state of filth and poverty. Hence, at present, the station of Outacamund, usually a health resort, is one of great infection. Bangalore, standing also high, is another, while the low-lying points in the Madras Presidency, including that city, have had no cases save those imported. We shall hope to reach and pass that region before it becomes epidemic, and before other countries declare quarantine against that section. If we are not successful in this, then we shall go north to the upper table-land, that of Delhi and Agra, where, strange to say, they have had no plague, though the weather is of course much colder than in Bombay.

When the rats and mice begin to die it will be known that the plague has arrived, and the mortality of the natives will be, as it always is, fearful.

One old man told me that he regarded the pest and cholera as punishments sent direct from God; that he believed it is not the will of the Creator that the doctors should discover a cure for either, or else after all their study they would have done so long since, but they have not, and the people die like sheep in the shambles. A statue of the Queen in Bombay was mutilated some few years ago by natives, and immediately the plague appeared and slew its thousands. That vandalism, he firmly believed, was the cause of its appearance. Of the 250,000 recorded victims in India, the Bombay Presidency is responsible for 134,000, and the record there is still 1000 per week,—the *recorded* deaths,—but the real number is far above that.

When the plague first broke out in Bombay, funerals were attended by all the relatives of the deceased, but, as it spread, thousands and tens of thousands fled the town. The railway station was beleaguered; the dead were left to the bearers—and the dead were thousands, for few, if any, escaped once that dread horror had seized upon them. Its attack was sudden, its work swift. In the English club at Poonah six servants died in one night. Major H—— told me that he was in a chemist's shop one day when a fine-looking Eurasian woman entered and asked for a drug. Then she suddenly dropped down and was dead before anything could be done for her.

To-day in Bangalore, the natives are dying by hundreds, leaving their dead under the fruit stalls and in old wells because of their dread of segregation and the risk to their castes which arises therefrom.

Many white people have also been stricken, but some of them do recover; as the pest is generally considered a disease of dirt the immunity of Europeans is attributed to cleanliness, and to the well-ventilated condition of their houses. Mice as a rule do not get the disease—rats do. Among the Hindoos the percentage of deaths is less on each floor up from the ground. The difficulty in cleansing the quarters of the poor arises from their intense desire for seclusion. Dr. Weir of Bombay (see *Times* of India, December 10, 1898) considers the spread of the disease to be due principally to the rats, and to articles of food and merchandise "infected by mice." He also thinks that well-to-do people are more apt to carry the disease than the poorer classes, but that the danger of infection is not so great through human beings as through merchandise. He believes that the disease is now epidemic in upper India and near the mountains. The poor are so constantly in the sun that their clothes are disinfected, while the reverse holds with the better classes. He considers that the pest is contracted from the abrasions between the toes, and that dirt and dust kill the microbes. Hence those "who walked in dust and lived in dirt" were less liable to be infected than those who avoided the dust and wore shoes. If dirt is a preventative why clean the houses? and why is the death-rate so much higher in such places and among the people "who walk in dust and live in dirt" than among the other classes? Apparently no two opinions concur as to the scourge, its origin, or cure.

The *Times* also states that "the course of the plague depended upon how the rats moved," and that more than fifty thousand rodents have been destroyed at Bombay. Twenty-five thousand people have been inoculated. They do not now object to the operation as much as at first, because the Government compensates them for the time lost while laid up with the fever. Pnumonic plague is the worst form of the disease. Lately a woman died of the pest after delivering a child, but the latter was quite free from any symptom of the disease.

The Government of India is certainly placed in a delicate and distressing position during the visitation of these scourges. To forbid the Hindoo method of burning—which never entirely consumes the body—would cause a riot, therefore when the epidemic was at its height, and hundreds of corpses were awaiting the sacred fire, the effect upon the living can easily be imagined. If a man is wealthy he is well burned. If not, such wood as can be paid for is furnished, and what is left of him is cast to the dogs, or the river, as I happened to see at Benares. As for the Parsis, they must be taken to the Towers of Silence, which, being but five in number, were totally inadequate to dispose promptly of the many dead brought there during the worst times in Bombay, and it is said that the waiting dead around them multiplied in an awful manner.

It is surprising to note how little is known about those Towers even in England. One of the great London illustrated papers, *The Graphic*, if I remember correctly, gave a full-page illustration of a "Scene at the Towers of Silence during the Plague." There was not a Parsi in all the groups of people before them. The Towers were represented as tall, square, and majestic structures, whereas they are low, circular buildings some twenty-five feet high and two hundred and seventy-six feet in circumference, and are whitewashed. A small door part way up the side gives ingress to the dead and its bearers, who alone ever enter these abodes of horror. The interior holds a circular grating some distance down from the top upon which the dead are laid, the men in the outer circles, the women next, and the children nearest the centre, where there is a well for the collection of the bones. The Towers stand upon Malabar Hill, the highest spot around Bombay. Beautiful gardens surround them where, it is stated, "the relatives sit and meditate in the sweet silence after their dead have passed away from their sight forever." But if they do they must be deaf, else they would be driven insane by the horrid shrieking and calling of the vultures, by the awful battles in high air, amid the branches of the trees, and indeed upon the ground before the people. Could there be a greater horror than this? Yet these Parsis are the last people that one would imagine could approve of such methods. They are, as a rule, handsome, the men fine-featured, large-eyed, and stately as to figure, the women very refined and pleasant to gaze upon.

Yonder stand two dark-eyed dames dressed in white cloth; a silk mantle of pale yellow with a black border is draped from the head and folded gracefully around the figure. They are a very bright, shrewd race, and are most intelligent talkers—an improved, healthy, and handsome edition of the Spaniards.

In the five Towers many dead can be taken care of under ordinary circumstances, but it was impossible to care for the hundreds slain by the plague. Thousands of vultures were drawn thither by the unusual state of affairs, and there can be little doubt that this method of disposing of the dead was a prime factor in spreading the pest. A chemist who lived in Bombay during the whole time told me that he saw a vulture drop a human bone into the compound of a bungalow, and that shortly afterwards nearly all of the native servants died of the plague.

What could the Government do under such circumstances? Earth, water, and fire being sacred to the Parsis, and hence not to be polluted by that most corrupt of all things, a dead body, what could be done with the dead?

A Parsi funeral is a solemn, stately procession consisting of the corpse, its bearers, and many mourners and friends, all dressed in white and walking two by two. The procession pauses by the house of prayer just inside the gates, and then passes onward to a sign beyond which none may pass save the dead and those four bearers, outcasts like the mummifiers of Egypt, who carry it upwards through that low door and out of sight forever. If it has once passed beyond that sign-post no one may stop it, be they ever so near and dear, and that passage must be to them as the sound of the falling clods is to us. One hears many tales—let us hope that they are but "tales"—of those who have been carried in there alive, never to come forth again.

What strange messenger carried to the vultures even in Turkestan the awful tidings of the dead? How did they know what was happening or about to happen in far Bombay, that they started on their flight southward, appearing finally on Malabar Hill in numbers never known before? Five or six hundred is their usual quota in that garden, but then they were countless, and the Towers had a border of black added to their summit as the vultures sat closely crowded together while awaiting their feasts—feasts that were not long in coming. It is claimed, however, by the Parsis that, no matter how great the number of the dead each morning, they were disposed of in a very short space of time, and that the idea that any fragment may have been "carried off and dropped," thereby spreading the contagion, is untrue, for the reason that when a vulture extends his wings in flying he must open his claws, and hence could not use them, and that he does not use his beak. Be that as it may, even the plague has not caused any change of ideas amongst the Parsis that will result in the abolition of this, to our thinking, objectionable mode of disposing of the dead.

But the shores of the mainland and the port of Tuticorin are in sight, and for better or worse we go forward.

NATIVE CART, MADURA.

CHAPTER III

MADURA

The Panorama of the Peoples of India—The Approach to Madura —The Feast to Shiva—The Gopuras—Courts, Sanctuaries— "Tank of the Golden Lilies" and the Starving Queen—The Sacred Elephants, Bulls, and Parrots—The Dirt of the Temple —Responsibility of the Sacred Tanks for the Cholera—Legends and Treasures of Madura.

THE panorama of the peoples of India never loses its attraction for the stranger within her borders. In China, in Java, in Japan, or in Turkestan there is a sameness in the multitude that gradually destroys one's interest, but it is never so in India. Each Presidency has its distinct types, and with each shifting of the scene some new picture is presented, different in every particular from the last. As we land, my attention is at once attracted by a band of dignified Mohammedans, waiting to take ship to Colombo, and thence to Mecca. Many wear the green turban of the Prophet. They disappear and are succeeded by a stately lot of white-robed Parsis, who withdraw themselves from the common crowd, while all the avenues beyond are filled with a steadily moving mass of Hindoos on their way to the shrines at Madura.

As our train moves along we are never out of sight of groups of them, and, as we approach the city, the throng becomes a multitude. Each shrine has its thousands of devotees, and the roads are choked with those who are moving onward to the festival of Shiva, under the shadows of those great gopuras rising so majestically yonder. Men and women of the lower castes are on foot; those of the higher ride on horseback, or in the quaint pagoda-like ox-carts of the land. Yonder is a rajah, or someone of degree, seated in state upon a gaily caparisoned elephant whose clanking bells cause the people to scatter right and left as he passes onward.

High on a rock burns a sacred fire, which must burn until the rains extinguish it. Along the passageway to the holy flame are many priests of this strange faith, instructing the people. But the multitude press onward, carrying us with them to the great shrine of the city.

What pen can picture Madura? Mounting to the roof of her royal palace, and gazing outward, the traveller beholds on all sides an ocean of waving palms with a gorgeous Indian city sheltered under their branches. The streets are thronged and all the people are in festal garb, crimson and scarlet predominating as to colour. Against a sky of saffron yellow the great gopuras (towers) of the temples soar aloft more than one hundred feet above the humbler dwellings, thousands of statues of the numberless gods crowding their pyramidal sides, while fantastically carved dragons toss their wings upward from the summits.

An encircling and jagged chain of mountains en-

ENTRANCE TO GREAT GOPURA, MADURA.

closes the valley of the city, reminding one of the volcanoes of Java.

As the shadows fall we approach the precincts of the temple. Myriads of lights begin to twinkle and the festival of Shiva commences. All the approaches to the structure are thronged. Dark figures swathed in white, moving silently and ghostly, or glowing in all the colours of the rainbow, press onward; the women so decked out with golden bangles that they dispense tinkling music as they crowd inward to where the sacred bull rests embowered in yellow flowers and encircled by blinking lights. Each devotee, on passing the graven image, reverently touches it with both hands, and then transfers the blessing to his lips, whence it is wafted to the abode of Shiva. Through an archway, glowing with countless lights which are never extinguished, stretch the dark corridors of the temple, a long vista of columns carved grotesquely in the forms of gods and animals, while in the farther distance, to which we may not penetrate, stands a golden Shiva adored by countless worshippers; and countless worshippers adored the god upon this same spot when our religion was but a prophecy to be fulfilled, for this portion of the temple is said to date back three centuries before Christ.

In the court of the "tank of the golden lilies" a live bull with gilded horns picks his way daintily among the lamps, which cluster like glow-worms on the steps. Silently the crowds make way for us, silently they close around and follow after us, the fitful torchlights showing their gleaming black eyes and dazzling teeth, while their wreaths of yellow flowers load the air with perfume. The swaying forms of the sacred elephants fill the background, their clanking bells sounding above the voices of the people. The scene is Eastern, Indian, idolatrous, and one never to be forgotten.

To-morrow we will return for a closer inspection, but it is well to have had this weird, fantastic glimpse of Madura in high fête in honour of the great god Shiva.

It is always pleasant to have a first view of these temples by moonlight or torchlight, as the full light of the day brings out all the dirt and filth which are forever attendant upon heathen shrines.

The visit to-day was most interesting. The temple of Madura ranks next in size to Rameswaram. It is a parallelogram of eight hundred by seven hundred feet. There are nine great gopuras, and there is a hall of a thousand columns. The "tank of the golden lilies" is surrounded by a colonnade gorgeously painted with representations of the most famous pagodas in India. On one side you will observe the little chapel of Queen Mangammal, who was starved to death in 1706, her subjects placing food so near that she could see and smell, but could not reach it. England has a like legend in the case of Richard II., in Pontefract Castle. Exquisite tortures have not been confined to the Orient.

We are greeted by the usual dense crowd of natives, who follow us everywhere. Sacred elephants, with foreheads painted in white, sway from side to side on either hand; their mahouts, on seeing us, suddenly mount to their seats and advancing down the corridors cause the beasts to kneel in salu-

STONE CARVINGS AT MADURA.

tation. The sensation of the one to whom the adoration is offered is peculiar to say the least. Many bananas are offered and promptly devoured. I give one beast a stalk which he rejects, while he waves his trunk in doubt over my head, but I allow him no chance to settle the matter. Sacred parrots chatter at us, and sacred bulls butt their way amidst the crowd, while a priest decorates us with garlands of yellow flowers. His caste would be outraged if he accepted less than a rupee for his attentions.

The carvings of this temple are most intricate and marvellous, but the temples of Southern India must not be compared with those of the Moslems, such as the mosque at Delhi and the Taj. They are barbarically grand as to their exterior, their towers, and their tanks, and grotesquely fantastic as to their corridors and carvings, but they are filthy inside. I know of no exception to this unless it be at Rameswaram, but at Madura the very columns are soaked in the grime and grease of ages. As for this "hall of a thousand columns," it is considered the most marvellous part of the temple, but it does not strike me as such. It is low and dark, and though some of the carvings are very remarkable, the majority are very crude, in fact of the crudest description, and it is all inexpressibly dirty. The water in the "tank of the golden lilies," some twelve feet deep, is a mass of green slime which must necessarily breed terrible diseases. Hindoos regard all the tanks as sacred, and their waters as blest by the gods, and therefore to be greatly sought after. They are undoubtedly the source from which cholera stalks forth, and, I doubt not, the plague also.

It seems as though the risk of such diseases, especially the cholera, would be greatly decreased by insisting upon the cleaning of these sacred tanks and cisterns, and by having a flow of water pass constantly through them. But, of course, the Government dislikes in any way to interfere with the religion of these people. Take, for instance, the sacred well at Benares. It scores its victims by the hundreds of thousands yearly, and might almost be called the birthplace of cholera. If a few lives, comparatively speaking, were saved by the suppression of the suttee, would it not be well to endeavour also to save the millions that yearly die from these "sacred waters"? Would it not be an added protection to all the world? for India sends the cholera outward to all nations.

Madura is surrounded by countless legends of the Hindoo faith. It was saved from Moslem destruction by Shiva's causing a stone bull to rise and consume some plantains, a sure demonstration that the Hindoo faith was the true one.

There are many treasures at this shrine, but the most interesting and important are the bulls, dragons, peacocks, palanquins, and platforms, all of solid gold and silver and encrusted with jewels. The idols are very large, and each has a day sacred to itself when it is carried in procession through the corridors of the temple.

Unfortunately, it rains heavily during our daylight inspection and we cannot examine the gopuras as thoroughly as we desire, but they are ever present; through every doorway and archway, and across every enclosure, they rear their beautiful structures

TANK OF THE GOLDEN LILIES MADURA.

high aloft, and travellers find that they never lose their charm, beauty, and majesty. The accompanying illustration gives a far better idea of their effect than any pen picture, however graphic.

We do not escape from the temple without further demonstrations on the part of the elephants. There is apparently an organised plot to head us off in all directions. Each corridor that we enter is blocked by a great dusky form, and when we least expect it a trunk is thrust in our faces demanding more bananas, but we notice above, back of the painted faces and waving ears, the dusky countenances of the mahouts, whose piercing black eyes are keen for rupees that may be scared from our pockets. It is the first time that I have ever played at "puss-in-the-corner" with bulls and elephants, while parrots of many hues act as umpires, and strange gods of carved stone, or moulded gold and silver, gaze stolidly upon me. The throngs of natives which follow and wall me in are less disagreeable, however, than many a collection of monks in Italy or crowd in America.

CHAPTER IV

TANJORE

The Palace of the Rajah—Its Pageants, Elephants, Musicians—The Splendours of a Durbar—The Palace Library and Hall of Audience—The Desolation of the Whole—The Pagoda of Tanjore—Its Stately Appearance and Superb Carvings in Stone—Its Stone Bull and Holy of Holies—The Minor Pagodas—The Passing of the Life and Wealth of Tanjore.

IN the days of its life, the court of the palace of the Rajah of Tanjore presented within its stately precincts a gorgeous pageant whenever His Highness held his durbars. In addition to the many elephants of his establishment, swaying and rocking at their chains, hundreds of others belonging to the courtiers crowded the spot, making the scene brilliant with their trappings, rending the air with their trumpeting and the clanging of their many bells. Their howdahs were gorgeous to behold, and their attendants gay as parrots in the livery of their masters.

Barbaric music from the royal players rose above the subdued murmurs of the crowd as the nobility of the land passed on under lofty arches to where His Royal Highness sat in state to receive them. With all his jewels blazing upon him he scarce out-

STATE PROCESSION OF ELEPHANTS, TANJORE.

shone the gorgeousness of many of his subjects, and the shadowy precincts of the Hall of Audience glowed with prismatic colours as the sunbeams pierced its twilight.

At its entrance, long rows of slippers, red and yellow, had been left by their owners before they passed into the presence of the Rajah, where they crowded both sides of the hall. The open space before the throne was occupied by girls who moved with a peculiar floating motion, keeping up a monotonous and low murmur of song which ever and anon rose into a weird incantation.

In the great library, the learned men of the palace pored over manuscripts in all known tongues, while from behind the lattice of the women's quarters came the sound of laughing voices. All was life and splendour.

How changed are the days at the palace! Into its great, empty court we rattle in bullock-carts, and draw up with much noise and little dignity at the arched entrance, where of old there were always a hundred elephants. Now there are two, one a young one that rebels at its loneliness, the other so old that its gaunt skull looks like a death's-head. Its small eyes are sunken almost out of sight, and its great frame sways wearily to and fro, as though anxious to be gone after all the others, dead now for many years. This one they say has passed its century, and could tell tales of much splendour, and of much horror, no doubt—for all was not sunshine for those who lived in the palace at Tanjore one hundred years ago. He shows his age as would an old man, and the weight of years is too much for him. He was once one of many that clanked their chains about this courtyard; he can remember grand processions, when the old Rajah came in state to the palace, when the howdahs glistened with jewels, when crimson, and cloth of gold, and gems ornamented his own huge bulk. Then, his forehead was painted like a Cashmere shawl, and his toes were gilded. He can remember the multitude that bowed before his prince as he bore him through yonder arch, and onward to the great pagoda, where the highest in the land were in attendance. But that is gone now—he is the last of his company; he has seen the vanishing of all that glittering throng.

The Hall of Audience stands unaltered, but is empty and deserted, save on the throne, where a marble statue of His Royal Highness holds forever its silent state. On the walls around hang the portraits of the long line of rajahs. Their eyes follow us, and instinctively we glance behind almost expecting to be called to account by some dusky attendant, but no sound breaks the silence of the empty palace. From the window of the Queen's court comes no sign of life, but as we pass onward the wild, barbaric music of the court musicians rends the air and tears the silence into tatters. Still it holds the notes of mournfulness, is full of a wail of sorrow over all that is gone forever into other courts, into other Halls of Audience, and we in turn depart, leaving the marble semblance of the ruler alone in the palace, save for the moonlight which streams in upon it, seeming to quicken the cold stone into full life.

DURBAR SALON, TANJORE.

It is often the case that the places about which one has heard the least prove to be the most impressive and interesting. This is true of the temple of Tanjore, which, to my thinking, is the most impressive, the most stately, in Southern India. The entire temple is of stone from the foundations to the highest point, whereas the most majestic portion of Madura, the gopuras, are of stone only in their lower stories, all the upper section being of plaster and stucco. The main pagoda of Tanjore rears its majestic outlines two hundred feet above the centre of an immense colonnade, under the arches of which are a vast number of shrines, while small temples flank the greater one on either side. The entire structure is a mass of beautiful carvings in bold relief, and the effect of the whole is wonderfully enhanced by the dark red of its sandstone, toned to a point of beauty which can only be accomplished by the flight of ages, and Tanjore is nine hundred years old. What a multitude of graven images! But the statues of these Hindoo gods do not impress one as do those of Buddha at Boero Boda; there is a smirk, and sometimes almost a grin, about these, which seems to indicate that they are well aware that they are not true gods—that they are in fact playing a part; while no one who has ever gazed upon the statues of Buddha can fail to be impressed with their majesty and dignity.

Another vast difference between the carvings of the Buddhists and the Hindoos lies in the fact that there is never any suggestion of the impure or obscene in the works of the former, whereas the Hindoos seem to revel in the depiction of all that is vile, especially upon their temples. I have to-day examined a photograph which shows the carvings upon some great gopura. Nothing viler or more obscene exists in any section of the world, but such does not appear to be the case at Tanjore.

This temple differs materially from other temples in one point. The gopuras elsewhere are mere entrances and gateways, answering to the propylons of Egypt, but here the gopura, though of the same general design, rises in the centre of the temple and covers the holy of holies. In other words, it is the temple proper before which crouches the stone bull, a majestic monolith in black marble, some twelve by fourteen feet, which possesses a pagoda of its own and rests upon a platform. What it sees in the darkness of the holy of holies we are forced to imagine, as we may not enter. In fact, nothing save the power of England renders our presence possible even in the outer courts of these heathen shrines. Murray tells us, however, that this shrine contains in the centre a huge black slab of marble which upholds the "lingam." There is also an image of Shiva facing south, while close by is the shrine of the god whose duty it is to report to the chief god the arrival of worshippers.

A thorough inspection of the carvings of Tanjore would occupy the traveller for weeks. Its smaller shrine, that of Karttikeya the son of Shiva and the deity of war, is considered to rival the great pagoda in its cut stone work, and is considered the most beautiful structure in Southern India. So it may be in detail, but the soaring majestic outlines of the greater structure are far more impressive and

GREAT PAGODA OF TANJORE.

attractive, and the eye returns again and again to its satisfying outlines. With the passing of the wealth and power of the rajahs, Tanjore lost its estates and income and, to-day, stands silent and deserted.

CHAPTER V

MADRAS

"The Forsaken of God"—The Indian and English City—The Vile Hotel, Bats, and Toads—The Cobra—Habits of the Serpents—Harbour of Madras—Teeming Life on its Beach—The People and Crows—Plague Inspection—Approach of the Pest—The Hand of England in India.

THE north-east monsoon is still raging as we approach the largest city of Southern India. All the land for miles around is covered with vast sheets of water, and the rain falls in driving torrents, while the ocean moans and thunders outside the bar. This harbour is so unsafe that ships have to put to sea at such times, and all up and down the Coromandel coast there is no port of refuge, from the mouth of the Ganges to where Cape Comorin faces the Indian Ocean. This is the region of cyclones, tornadoes, and tidal waves. One associates such names as Pondicherry and Madras with all that is fearful and awful in the elements, and now, combined with the god of storms, the skeleton of the "Black Death" is surely advancing upon all this section of the land, justifying the title which the English have given to the city of Madras—"the forsaken of God."

STONE BULL (MONOLITH), TANJORE.

Like all Anglo-Indian cities, Madras, with a population numbering four hundred thousand, covers a territory about equal to that of a city of five times its population. Its appearance from the sea is imposing and majestic, as all the great Government buildings are stretched along the esplanade, and from the tower of the municipal building a brilliant light shines by night far out over the tossing waters. Vast commons stretch backward from the shore, and "Black Town," the old city, is close by the river, which separates as it nears the sea. In order to reach the residential portion of the city one crosses these arms on three fine bridges.

The English section possesses very wide and immensely long avenues bordered with fine trees, which, in season, must present a gorgeous sight, as many are *Poinciana regias.* All the houses stand well back in large compounds full of trees and shrubs, the general appearance being fine, though in detail such is not the case. Travellers fail to understand the philosophy of the domestic English architecture in Southern India. Though a land of enormous rainfalls and of great dampness, it is the custom to build a house flat on the ground with no sort of cellar nor chance for ventilation underneath. My room in this most wretched hotel, the Elphinstone, is raised above the mud outside only by the thickness of its cement floor, which is all cracked and mouldy. I fully expected to have last night's deluge flood the whole apartment. A mouldy matting covers the cement, while the plaster of the dripping walls is green with mould. The bath-room is infinitely worse, but one does not have to sleep therein. Bats fly around my head as I write, and a constant soft pat, pat, over the floor causes me to make an inspection with the lamp, whereupon dozens of small toads hop off into corners from which they regard me with a serious mien, approaching a little nearer now and then—but one does not mind toads!

Madras is noted for its cobras, and I confess that I spend a half-hour in stopping up all possible means of ingress for that most beautiful of serpents. It is sacred with the Hindoos because, upon discovering one day in the desert a newly born son of one of the gods, whose life would soon have passed away under the fierce rays of the rising orb, a cobra coiled itself near the babe, raised its head, and distended its hood, thus making itself all day long to that baby as is the "shadow of a great rock in a weary land" to the traveller. But, in these latter days, it brings death and not life to those it approaches. These serpents always go in pairs, and if you kill one you may be sure that its mate will track it. Therefore be on guard for your life. There are no serpents in this beastly room to-night, however; still I barricade against all possible enemies, and tucking the curtains in securely, sleep until tea is brought in at daylight.

In the present condition of the country a man in Madras is, as it were, in a pocket. Quarantine may be declared any day, and I hasten to get off on the ship to Rangoon.

There is no harbour at Madras. The waves roll in between two stone breakwaters and thunder on the beach beyond, so embarkation is no easy matter, and I see that I am to have another sensation during the process—travel in the East is made up of sensations. The sands swarm with a motley concourse of beings, most of them without clothes. Men, women, and children live here all their lives and everything goes on in plain air. It strikes one as decidedly odd to see grave-looking crows amid such a crowd,—black, with a grey mantle, they are veritable preachers in appearance,—but a Madras crow is not a priest nor anything else that savours of divine. Of all the crows in India he is deemed the most impudent and the greatest thief. He knows what he wants, and whether or not his right may be upheld by law, he takes it. If you stop him he assumes an insulted look and jabs at you. During my passage to the water I have been treated in this manner several times by crows that I happened to disturb. They said but little, but they meant what they said, which is perhaps much more than can be claimed for many of our lawmakers under the dome of the Capitol.

The traveller can reach his ship only by means of a great, clumsy surf-boat or hulk some twenty feet long by eight broad and five deep, shaped like the half of a cocoanut. Such a craft cannot, of course, be drawn up high and dry, as it would be impossible to float it again; therefore, after my luggage has been dumped aboard, two dirty blacks approach and, *sans* ceremony, grab me by the legs and elbows and proceed seaward. Dirt or no dirt, plague or cholera, under such circumstances one clings like death, until the side of the barge is reached, where for an instant one balances between mud and dirty water inside, and sharks and clear water outside. In my case the balance is settled in favour of the former by a black who seizes my feet and hauls me inward. Some twenty or thirty men rush into the water, lay hold of the lumbering craft, and roll us into the surf. That it does not upset is a miracle, but once at sea it proves very steady, and I am soon on board ship.

The inspection by the port doctor was a mere form, and I have no doubt that he is often deceived. He asked me where I came from and took my word for it, and merely touched the wrist of my servant, certainly not long enough to discover whether or not he had fever. However, as yet, Madras has not been infected and all ports are open to her, but as I look forth from my safe harbour on this ship I wonder how long or how short the time will be before the stalking spectre of death shall cast its shadow on her sky, before the rats begin to die, and the people to vanish like the mists of the morning. In the south, the death-rate among the white people has been much greater than in the north, though they can fight a better battle than the natives and sometimes recover. Under the circumstances I confess that I am glad to quit India.

It is at all times a pleasure to note with how firm but kind a hand England governs these peoples. She has learned only through sad experience, but she has learned, and to-day all the millions of the land live more contentedly and in greater accord than they have ever done. Let us hope for the sake of humanity that her rule will never end, for she would certainly lose her place among the great nations if she lost India, and chaos would ensue throughout that land.

CHAPTER VI

BAY OF BENGAL

Passage of the Bay—Dangers of an Insufficient Provision for an Accident—Native Crowds under Deck—Life of a Saloon Passenger on these Ships—Edison and Omdurman—English Opinion of that $20,000,000 Paid for Manila—Cholera on Board—Prospect of Quarantine—Landing at Rangoon.

S. S. *Putiania*, BAY OF BENGAL, December 2, 1898.

GIVEN a small ship of twenty-eight hundred tons, and possessing but eight medium-sized boats, load the craft with two thousand coolies in addition to her first- and second-class passengers and her crew, and one has the elements for a terrible tragedy if an accident should occur. Such boats as could be lowered would not carry a fraction of the human freight aboard this ship. It is horrible even to think of the scene that would ensue, and one could only hope that God in His mercy would send the craft swiftly to the bottom. There should be a law against such overcrowding, and yet when the captain is interrogated his answer comes promptly in the form of a question: "What great Atlantic liner carries enough life-saving apparatus to save her human freight?" None do so, as I was forced to confess, yet I fancy that most of the lines would insist that they send out their ships well equipped for any emergency.

As I look down on the lower decks yonder, the mass of wriggling, seething blacks resembles a den of serpents. How utterly unmanageable and how terrible they would be if the slightest cause for commotion occurred! They are on the way to Burma to work in the rice-fields, and will receive a rupee each (thirty-two cents) per day as against one quarter of the sum in India. There are many women among them, and they all live, eat, and sleep pell-mell down there, while on a raised hatch in their midst my servant, together with those of several English officers on board, holds his state separate and apart. Yonder is a black woman with rings on toes and fingers; she wears also anklets and bracelets, earrings and necklaces, all of gold and silver, while her black baby sits on a box, destitute of all clothing, but laden with jewelry. These people carry their wealth in that way, and are often murdered for the treasure.

Near the mother and child are some Nautch girls whom we have vainly endeavoured to induce to dance for us, and beyond is a wriggling, kicking mass of scantily clothed men, whose black eyes gleam snakelike in the half-light under the awning. I cannot study them as closely as I should like, as every one of the four thousand eyes appears riveted upon my face, especially the pair belonging to a maiden at the foot of the steps. The men, as a rule, wear only a breech-cloth, while the women drape themselves in one long garment, which they manage to wrap in a graceful manner about their persons.

The women are not unpleasant in appearance, and one cannot but feel deeply sorry for them. Yonder are two little girls, one twelve and the other eight years of age, both bright, pretty, and intelligent children, and apparently well educated for their years, but what sad fates await them! The elder is already married, and will go to her husband when she reaches her fourteenth year. He is past fifty—such matches are common—and will of course leave her a widow long before we should consider a woman as fully matured. According to Hindoo laws she cannot remarry, and there is no future for her. She will probably do as many of her sex in this Eastern land have done—enter a life of shame, very likely in the house of some Brahmin.

Life on these ships is generally pleasant for the traveller. I have as companions in the saloon three English officers, also a Scotch broker of Rangoon—all agreeable, intelligent men. Most of the time is passed in listening to yarns of army life in the far colonies of the British Empire, or else just doing nothing, lazily ensconced in long cane chairs.

Will it be news to our wizard, Edison, to know that he had largely to do with the success of England in the battle of Omdurman, where Gordon was at last avenged? So it would certainly appear, as it is stated that the search-lights used by the English completely disorganised the forces of the Mahdi, so far as the night attack was concerned.

I remarked to Major H——, who related the circumstance:

"You see you cannot get along without America."

"God bless you, man, we don't want to," was the reply.

The report comes now that our Government has offered Spain $20,000,000 for the Philippines. There is general indignation amongst the English officers over our doing so, and one remarks, "Why pay her a d—d dollar? How many do you think we would pay her under the circumstances?" But a truce to grave subjects—they are not for such air as this.

It is most unusual to see any animal life as one passes over the ocean, but to-night as I watch the sun go down over the Bay of Bengal, across the broad river of crimson cast by his dying rays slowly passes a great black shark, his dorsal fin and tail cutting the waves like the keel of a boat.

Major H—— comes up behind me as I call his attention to the glory of the departing day.

"Bosh, talk of the sunsets at sea! It is the sunsets over Piccadilly that I admire, and the beauties of nature that walk the streets. I am sick of sunsets after thirty years in India."

Has the dreaming mind any power of connection with, or knowledge of, passing events? All last night I was troubled with dreams of death and funerals, and on awakening this morning was informed of two deaths during the night among the coolies, both caused by cholera, and followed by prompt burials in the sea. This may mean a quarantine of endless duration for the ship, for if cholera has broken out among that seething mass below, God alone knows what the end will be, or whether any of us will escape to tell the tale. It is not a cheerful outlook and we are very grim over it as we see the fatal yellow flag hoisted to the foremast. What will the port doctor say? (These ships carry no physicians of their own.) Yonder tug will settle the matter, and we wait with a hopeless kind of patience.

Evidently cholera is not dreaded as is the plague, for after an inspection of the coolies, the ship moves onward, and we land with no detention whatever, save what is occasioned by those who pause to utter a fervent "Thank God," as we reach terra firma and are free.

CHAPTER VII

BURMA

First View of the Great Pagoda—Sarkie's Abominable Hotel and the Fight therein—Clubs and Parks of Rangoon—English Section—Value of Burma — Season for Travel — Departure for Karthay—Cool Air of the Irrawaddy—Sail to Bhamo, and Approach to China—Teak Forests—The Elephant at Work—Sagacity and Strength—Cost of a Healthy Beast—Bhamo—Its Trade with China—Ancient Joss-House.

FROM the long line of the Himalayas as they stretch east and west across the continent of Asia several ranges of mountains run southward into the peninsula of farther India. A spur divides that peninsula into two sections, the westward half, bound north and east by these mountains, and south and west by the Bay of Bengal and India, forming what is called by man "Burma," a land noted for its teak-woods, its rice, carvings, and lacquer-work—a land of commerce and Eastern romance.

As the traveller approaches from the sea, the coast shows low and sandy, and slowly encompasses our ship as she steams up the muddy Irrawaddy; but long before the land evolves itself from the water the great pagoda of Rangoon, catching the light of the morning sun, gleams like a cone of gold rising from an ocean of mist. As our ship draws nearer we find that the temple stands on the top of a hill around whose base the foliage of the tropics rolls its leafy waves.

Along the water-front the city presents some shapely buildings, and the stream is filled with a goodly number of craft, European and Asiatic. To the newly arrived traveller Rangoon is a disappointment, and at first sight the one word "rickety" describes it better than could be done by a volume of six hundred pages. Many buildings are of brick, but dusty and slovenly in the extreme. The hotels are an abomination. "Sarkie's," which is called the best, would in dirt and squalour put to shame any of the hotels of India, or the worst post-houses of Transcaspia. The orgies which go on there after dark are a disgrace to the authorities that allow such a state of affairs. Coming in about midnight on Monday, and expecting semi-quiet at least, our ears were greeted by a tumult from the dining-room, which, increasing momentarily, lasted until three o'clock. No licence for the sale of liquors is required here, and they sell all night. Each of these establishments possesses a barmaid, and the one at Sarkie's had ascended from below stairs, celebrating her entrance by striking an unoffending man over the head with a soda-water bottle. A fight ensued and raged all over the place. In any other spot on the globe the police would have put a quick ending to the affair and closed the house, but I am told that these police, being all natives, would not dare to arrest a European. Scarcely credible under British rule! It was hours before those of us who were forced to stop at Sarkie's knew what quiet was. The whole establishment is a disgrace to the place.

It is not agreeable to be obliged to make such a statement, but perhaps it may do some good. It is pleasant on the other hand to render thanks for the attention and hospitality of those with whom it has been my good fortune to travel, and who have made these few days bearable. The "Jymkhana" Club is a pleasant spot and full of agreeable people, and the open-hearted hospitality of the English here causes one to forget all that is disappointing.

As the day declines we drive to a very beautiful park with some lovely lakes therein. It will stand comparison with most of the parks in Europe, and the view from the pavilions, comprising the lakes with their border of tropical foliage, the distant prospect over the surrounding country, and the great pagoda, soaring high in the heavens and glittering like a vast stately lighthouse, is certainly unique of its kind.

As the boat club is out to-night, the scene is very animated, and were it not for the palms and yonder group of yellow-robed priests, we might fancy ourselves in Europe.

Rangoon is laid off in very wide avenues shaded by handsome trees. The houses are undoubtedly the best for the place and climate, though at first they strike a foreigner as odd, to say the least. They are all raised on stilts and are of open work to a degree most amazing to those not accustomed to such publicity in a dwelling.

Of course, dust soon arises no matter how wet the

season has been, and all Rangoon looks dusty now, though the "rains" are not a month past, and the "rains" this year meant almost a downpour from April to November.

Considering the fact that England has had complete control of Burma only since 1885, the results already attained in the development of the country are marvellous, and will repay her a millionfold. Burma is a very rich country and is one of the largest producers of rice. Her resources are such that in the opinion of some authorities it is probable that in time she will be of more value to England than even India. It is stated that a lack of capital is the great drawback here, and that fifteen, twenty, and even thirty per cent. can be obtained for money with the best security offered as collateral, but the greater part of mankind regard Burma as being beyond the end of the world. The railroad into China will probably bring a large trade from that country.

This is the best season here; the nights are cool and comfortable, and the days are not unbearably hot. It has been said that Burma is "ten degrees hotter than hell." It may be so in the summer, but it is pleasant now.

These people possess strongly marked Chinese characteristics, and it would, therefore, be impossible for me to find anything charming in the women about whom one hears so much. I am told that the pure types are to be found in the upper country, and so I will suspend judgment. They are considered clever, and are the "business men," so to speak, of the family. If you contract with a carpenter it is his wife who carries on the negotiations. All the dwellings, native and European, bear the Chinese stamp, the thick walls of India having disappeared.

Our train starts up country at 6 P.M. We have decided to go through to Karthay and Bhamo and to stop at Mandalay on the way down. It will take thirty-six hours, as the distance to Karthay is some six hundred and fifty miles. The dust is frightful; it covers everything by morning, and would be unbearable were the nights not cool. As it is, we sleep well.

The mountains are not visible until the day is well advanced, the landscape presenting a vast level plain covered with dusty acacia trees. It would almost appear as if, in the centuries past, some genii had passed over Burma and strewn it with countless bells, great and small, whose handles rear themselves by thousands in every direction. Like all other Buddhist pagodas, these are solid and are supposed to contain some relic. They stand singly or in large groups, some old and grey, some white and new—many in ruins. It is not considered meritorious to repair a pagoda, but decidedly so to build one, hence the vast and constantly increasing numbers of the sacred structures. It is a great drawback, however, to the interest of the traveller when he finds that these pagodas are all substantially alike, and that to have seen the best is to have seen all. This is not the case with the Indian temples, where no two are alike, but in Burma the traveller soon comes to regard them simply as a picturesque addition to the landscape.

As the train passes north, the mountains close in upon us in a long yellow chain, like unto those of the Valley of the Nile. Yellow rivers roll their sluggish waters seaward, and all along their banks stretch the matting walls of the native houses, each with its bunch of pagodas, making the scene most picturesque.

Our long railroad ride ends at Karthay, where we board a small river boat such as are used for post-boats on the Nile. There are four comfortable cabins and a pleasant deck with easy-chairs, all delightful to our tired bodies after the rough jolting of the train. The Irrawaddy stretches yellow and sluggish before us, and as we advance slowly it curves between low-lying banks. If the distant mountains were yellow the resemblance to Egypt's sacred river would be most marked.

The air has become so cool and fresh that our top-coats are in order. We are not so far from the great Himalayas, whose vast snow-fields must temper all the air of upper Burma. This is the country of great game, and it is not uncommon for the telegraph poles to be knocked over by elephants, or for a royal tiger, of which the forests hold thousands, to bound away through the dense jungle as the iron horse rushes around a curve. So far, neither in Southern India nor in Burma have we seen any monkeys, whereas in Northern India they abound both in towns and country.

The banks of the Irrawaddy are covered with a dense and very tall growth of pampas-grass with its plume-like flowers waving snowy and pure above it. Ever and anon the canoes of the natives shoot out from some cool creek with a swiftness worthy of the Indians of the St. Lawrence, whilst amidst every thatched village, and often high on the mountains, rise the sacred pagodas; some are gold and some pure white, but most of them are grey and ancient-looking, and, to my thinking, much more beautiful to look upon than the more brilliant structures.

We have reached once more the land of flowers, and yonder garden is full of a reign and a ruin of roses. There are those simple old home flowers, the marigolds, sacred to a garden such as each of us holds dear, where one's mother wandered amidst her roses and marigolds long ago in our better and purer days. How life changes with us all! How much we have to remember, and how much to regret, and how the perfume of a flower, or the glint of the gold of the marigold, brings it all back to us!

The air here is full of freshness, every breath being charged with life and health—a wonderful change from the languid, heavy atmosphere of Rangoon. In fact, the atmosphere at the sea-level in the tropics produces a nameless horror, a sense of boding ill, and forces one to realise that one is mortal.

We are evidently approaching the confines of the Celestial Empire. The roofs of the houses begin to turn upwards at the corners, while the ridge-pole sinks a little in the middle. The eyebrows of the people slant more towards the temples, the noses of the women are flatter, and those boatmen yonder boast no clothing save a vast straw hat shaped like a mushroom, which acts as an equal protection against sun and rain. The race is apparently a healthy and happy one, and as every house stands

UPPER IRRAWADDY, BURMA.

high above the ground I fancy they are spared many of the ills which attack the people of India who live down in the dirt. The pagodas have lost the bell shape of the south, and are composed of many roofs, one above the other, each smaller than the one below, and on that one in the distance a Chinese dragon flaunts in all its glory and gorgeousness. A flight of steps leads from the river to the main portal of the structure, and the noonday sun lights up the blazing coronet of an alabaster Buddha, while the sounds of sacred gongs float softly outward over the waters.

The forests have changed completely, all the palms and bamboos have vanished, all the flaming flowers of the tropics have disappeared. Yonder cool wood might be of the temperate zone; the mountains are a deep blue in colour, and the clouds have a rain-washed look and seem to hold snow in their bosoms. As evening approaches the air is full of the fragrance of pine trees straight from the region of falling waters, while the rays of the setting sun send long golden shafts through the aisles of the stately forests, and the wild clematis casts its snowy bridal wreaths from branch to branch. Great rafts of teak-wood drift slowly past us, steered by some of these little people. The forests from which the wood is cut are much higher up than Bhamo, the trees still remaining in this section being strictly preserved by the Government.

The teak is a very large and stately tree with a clean trunk for seventy feet before its branches spread outward. The forest grants are from the Government, and trees of only a certain size are allowed to be cut. Elephants are used in the hauling to the rivers, and sometimes thirty of these great beasts are harnessed to a single tree, which may measure some forty-five feet in length. This length is governed by the height of the water. Elephants are brought all the way from Moulmein below Rangoon, and take five months to reach the mountain forests. An elephant is trained to his work by hunger, a year being consumed in the teaching. It is quite possible to teach a full-grown beast captured in the forests.

There would seem to be small necessity for introducing steam or electric power into certain departments of trade in Burma. In the lumber business, for instance, aside from the sawmill, there are other forces which are cheaper and perhaps better than the modern inventions. Elephants are used most successfully, and it is a strange sight to see those enormous beasts quietly working away, using their great power in the moving, piling, and sorting of the great teak-woods. In one yard in Rangoon there are nine at work. Their actions are almost human, and there appears to be a perfectly understood system of signals, composed of guttural words and strokes of a stick, between the beast and his rider, who sits perched aloft on a seat like a sawbuck, and who guides his charge by gentle taps of the stick and of his heel. His slightest motion seems perfectly comprehended by the elephant, as perfectly as a "high-school" horse understands the wishes and motions of his rider.

Yonder are two engaged in piling timber which must first be drawn from the mud into which the

ELEPHANTS AT WORK, RANGOON.

receding tide has sunk it. An elephant is stationed at each end, and after one has lifted his end from the ground by inserting his tusks under it, he wraps his trunk around it and holds it high enough to allow the beast at the other end to get his tusks and trunk at work, when in concert they move forward and place the timber in its proper place. Timber after timber is so deposited, each evenly placed so that the completed pile, which rises as high as the beasts themselves, is a regular, symmetrical cube. Then the elephants stalk softly away, some to enter the water after stray logs, others to drag the sawn timbers away from the mill. This is done in several ways: sometimes by a collar around the neck to which traces are attached, but often the beast seizes a rope in his mouth, this is attached to a chain the other end of which is wrapped around the timber, and so it is dragged alongside the elephant's body, and never once does it get on his toes.

I notice that with some of the beasts the tusks appear sensitive, and then the trunk is used as a buffer between them and the timber. Why the trunk is not pierced is a mystery, but it does not seem to be injured in the least. As I stood watching one at work, I had a practical illustration of the silence with which they move. Something touched me lightly on the shoulder, and glancing backward I saw a huge beast quietly waiting for me to get out of the way. I really think that if it had been possible he would have gone around me, but as he was dragging three great pieces of timber, each at least twenty feet long and a foot thick, he awaited my pleasure, and I promptly indicated it to him by moving with a jump, it seemed to me, ten feet or more. He was an ancient and kindly old gentleman, with the same twinkling expression that I have often observed in gentlemen of his age, but not of his size. As he passed onward he flapped his great ears in salutation, regarding me solemnly the while.

The strength of these beasts is marvellous, and when put in force at the end of a timber, that timber moves, no matter what bars its progress; yet just here comes in one of the greatest evidences of the intelligence of the worker. Yonder is one shoving a heavy timber towards the sawmill. He evidently believes in husbanding his strength, for, finding the log badly hampered by others around it, he mounts the pile and sorts them out in a dignified manner. Seemingly he has eyes all around him, as he makes no false steps and his hind legs appear to know just where they should be placed. One can watch the working of these elephants for hours with interest.

A fine, healthy animal costs some forty-five hundred rupees, and no good one can be bought for less than three thousand. After the year's instruction very little trouble is experienced with them. There is one here that, when he is weary, simply lifts off his rider, and no amount of coaxing will induce him to do more work that day. This firm employs two hundred beasts in the forests, and last year they lost thirty through sickness, anthrax being the most prevalent disease. A healthy beast will often die during the night. They are generally worked until 10 A.M., and then for two hours in the afternoon. As the female has no tusks, she is not as serviceable as the male, but excels in intelligence, in which faculty she resembles her human sisters.

Navigation on the Irrawaddy is of a primitive character. The boats are run only during the day, as the slightest approach of night completely upsets the pilot, or else his position on the under deck obscures his sight of the course. At all events, he has run us aground once, and through two bamboo rafts, whose poles came rattling about us like hail in summer. Why the paddles were not destroyed is incomprehensible, as the bamboo is very tough and difficult to break. The raftsmen appeared to care very little and had little to say, nor did they lend the least assistance in extracting their flotilla. It was done at last and went drifting off into the darkness between the high cliffs which have closed in on the river. The landing for the night is shortly reached, our craft moored to the bank, and its human cargo sinks into slumber.

Daylight shows the morning mists lying so thickly over the river and hills that the steamer is unable to start before nine o'clock, and even then is forced to anchor in midstream once or twice, but the sun's rays are too strong for the vapours, and we are enabled to resume our journey. Our arrival at Bhamo will be delayed, but it matters not, as that place contains nothing of interest, being simply the farthest northern point to which the steamers run at present. It is in sight as I write. The valley of the river has spread out into a circle some twenty miles in diameter, enclosed by a chain of mountains not more than three thousand feet in altitude at the highest peak.

The left bank of the stream presents a curious sight just at present. A concourse of buzzards have selected that side for a bath, and great is the commotion. As each bird emerges from the water it hops away, and, turning its back to the sun, stretches its wings to their utmost in order to dry the feathers. It is a very odd sight to see whole rows of these great birds standing in this wise like huge bats, and not at all disturbed by the steam whistle.

Bhamo is the most northerly point in Burma where England has a military post. It is some fifteen miles from China on the east, but Burma extends two hundred miles farther northward. Caravans from China come to Bhamo to load and unload, but when the railroad is completed the trade of Burma with the Celestials is expected to increase greatly. Even now Bhamo is quite a trading point. It contains about nine thousand inhabitants, most of whom are Chinese.

There are very few pagodas here, and none of any interest or importance, but there is quite an interesting Chinese joss-house standing within an old Burmese fort. On either side of the gateway are the figures of an armed warrior holding his horse. The old joss-house is immediately within the gates and contains some curious images. Among them are two colossal figures of the good and evil genii. Beyond and behind is the new temple where Buddha, in alabaster, sits in high state with ten ingeniously modelled figures on either side, while small figures abound overhead and all around. Every section of the temple, old and new, is coloured to that point of gorgeousness so dear to the Oriental; the decorating of this inner shrine cost some fifty thousand rupees (about $16,000) and was done by the best artisans of China.

CHAPTER VIII

IRRAWADDY AND MANDALAY

Down the Irrawaddy—The Steamboats—Scenery *en Route*—The Mingun Pagoda—Approach to Mandalay—Appearance of the Outer Town—Cleanly Appearance of the People—The "Fort" —Burials Alive under its Walls—The "Jars of Oil" and their Portent—The Golden Palace—Pavilion of Audience and Dragon Throne—King Theebaw—Upper Burman Club—Palace of the Queen—The Lily Throne Room and the Murders which Occurred there—Life at the Club—Military Smoking Concert in the Open—Mandalay Hill—Temple of the "Seven Hundred Pagodas"—Sacred White Elephants—State of the King—Ploughing of the Fields—Fears of Usurpation—Burial of the King.

NOW we start southward down the sacred river until Prome is reached. It would be a difficult task to describe the fantastic panorama of that thousand miles. The steamer we board at Bhamo is an express boat, and much superior to the small craft which brought us here. It has large cabins and a large dining-room enclosed by Venetian blinds. There are electric lights and all that is needed for the traveller's comfort.

Our start downward is under the most propitious circumstances—no fog. The mountains of the Celestial Empire rise clear and sharp against the bright blue sky, and the long winding stream glitters in the ever-increasing sunlight. Crowds of natives squat along the banks and gravely regard our departure. The Chinese have no more expression than a wooden image, yet the race has a mysterious attraction, and their vast empire is interesting to explore. On the farther side of that broad chain of mountains the traveller would find many Janizaries, and all that strange, mystic life of the Chinese and Thibetans—but our way lies southward.

The first gorge below Bhamo presents some very fine scenery, which we passed in the night on the way up. The Irrawaddy narrows to a few hundred feet, and, at one point, passage seems impossible, the channel being so contracted. The climax is reached in a towering precipice which rises grandly upward from the river's edge. Near its base, on the pinnacle of a detached rock, is perched a small pagoda, its golden pyramid and scarlet base standing out against the dark green background and glowing in the sunlight. This air is delightful, and, if forced to live here in Burma, I should certainly make frequent pilgrimages up the river where every breath is full of vigour for body and mind.

It does not take long to reach the hot lowland, and after passing Karthay one feels again the tropical air full of languour and sleep. The disposition to walk vanishes with the cool breath of the mountains, and deck-chairs are again in demand.

The river grows wider and wider as we approach Mandalay. Pagodas stud more thickly the banks of the stream, and, some nine miles above the capital, the vast masses of the Mingun Pagoda are to be seen, picturesquely placed on a knoll above the river. Its huge, misshapen bulk covers a square of four hundred and fifty feet, its height being but one hundred and fifty-five feet, or about one third of what was intended, but the work was never completed and an earthquake rent the huge structure into many fissures. It is the largest mass of brick-work in the world, but the late King Mindohn Min attempted to surpass it. He commenced the construction of a pagoda which was to have been built of stone; whole hills were called upon to furnish the materials, and canals miles long were built to convey the blocks to the spot. A French engineer stated that with five thousand men working every day, eighty years would be required for its completion. After four years of labour, during which the foundations were completed, the work was abandoned, and with everything connected with it stands a ruin to-day, just to the east of Mandalay under the Shan Hills.

The mountains lose their stately forests and much of their height as the steamer nears the capital, so that the approach to Mandalay is not impressive. It would be difficult to make an impressive scene out of muddy waters, sand-banks, and barren hills. The sand-banks are the enemy of navigation on the Irrawaddy, and suddenly arrest our steamer's progress when she is within a mile of the landing-stage, holding her fast for two hours, so that it is long past noon when we land in the aforetime royal city of King Theebaw.

It is hot and dusty as we drive away from the

water, and heat and dust both increase until the desire to return to the steamer almost overpowers the desire to see this famous city. By the courtesy of Major H—— I am "put up" at the Upper Burman Club, and shall not have to endure the hotel, which, from report, is the worst in Burma.

Forty years ago this city of Mandalay did not exist, its site being a vast swamp and jungle. Then a royal edict appeared, after a consultation of the stars by the astrologers, commanding the removal of the capital from Amarapura some twelve miles away. Death was the penalty to all who refused, save in the case of the Chinese. Fear of the British Empire, and probably of that of China also, caused the King Mindohn Min to abandon the project so far as the Celestials were concerned, but all others promptly obeyed the edict. Down came stately palaces and straw huts, and all were soon erected where we see them to-day, thus forming Mandalay, the "City of Gems." Love of trade, however, brought all the newcomers among the Celestials to the new capital, and all the substantial houses therein belonged at first to either Chinese or Moguls, the natives having no right to erect any save those of straw.

The streets of Mandalay are very wide and not paved in any way, the result being, as already stated, that the dust is suffocating as we drive to the "fort." The shops and houses on either side do not present an attractive appearance, and the traveller wonders whether these are not merely the suburbs of the city, until a sudden turn in the avenue brings the "fort" into full view. That, he knows, is the very heart of Burma, so this must be the main portion of the outer city of Mandalay, and thus it proves.

One thing strikes the passer-by most favourably. Unlike most Eastern towns there are no bad odours, and "Yoe" * tells us this is owing to the vast number of scavenger dogs and of swine. As for the people, though not so interesting to look upon as in the days of Theebaw, they still form a very motley collection drawn from all the races of this section of the world. These streets are to-day full of a varied and ever-changing panorama, but old habits and laws are difficult to overcome, and the life and bustle fall back and away as we approach the entrance to the royal enclosure.

Travellers on their way to the club will enter at once upon the scenes connected with the fall of Mandalay and the surrender of King Theebaw. His royal city, now called the "fort," together with all the buildings which were once the scene of his luxurious court life, is now in daily use for the branches of the British Government of Mandalay. The fort might be called the "Kremlin" of Burma, but in size it would contain several of the Russian citadel. It is a square of a mile and a half each way, surrounded by a deep moat one hundred and fifty feet wide which is crossed by five bridges. In the royal days, before 1885, state barges floated upon the waters of this moat, but to-day nothing breaks the placid surface save countless lotus pads bearing aloft their pink and purple blossoms.

The entire square inside the moat is encompassed

* *The Burman: His Life and Notions*, by "Shway Yoe" (Stuart).

WALLS OF "THE FORT," MANDALAY.

by a brick wall fully thirty feet high and deeply denticulated its entire length. The bricks of this wall are of a dark red colour and are laid flat, apparently without mortar or cement. Over the twelve entrances rise fantastic, many-storied towers, and it is in connection with this wall and its gates and towers that the traveller encounters his first reminder of the horrible cruelties and barbarous superstitions of the old Burmans.

The land has possessed many royal cities since the days of old Pagahn, and human sacrifices were considered to sanctify and protect a new capital. Therefore when Mandalay was commenced, in 1858, fifty-two persons of both sexes and all ages were buried alive, three under each of these twelve gates, one under each of the four corners, one under each of the palace gates, and at the corners of the timber, or inner stockade, and four under the throne itself. The victims were persons of position, the boys could have no tattoo marks, the ears of the girls must not be bored. When it became known that the selection was being made the city became deserted. The Government gave great entertainments, all unattended, but the "tale" was at last completed.

Four jars of oil were also buried, one at each corner of the city, carefully covered and protected. They were examined every seven years, and so long as they remained intact the capital was considered safe. In 1880, it was discovered that two of these jars had become empty. Small-pox had carried off two of the King's sons, a great crown ruby had disappeared, and the royal tiger had escaped from its cage, a sure sign that the town would soon be turned into a wilderness.

Something must be done; Mandalay had become too substantial to be moved or abandoned, and it was decided to make human sacrifices of "a hundred men, a hundred women, a hundred boys, a hundred girls, a hundred soldiers, and a hundred foreigners." The panic in Mandalay became so great that the city was threatened with depopulation. Fright at the indignation of England caused the King and his ministers to countermand the edict, but it is claimed that people were buried alive under each of the posts at these twelve gates. All this happened less than twenty years ago. Truly we do not have to turn to the Dark Ages to look for horrors.

The cornices of all these towers, as well as all the royal buildings of the fort, are of beautifully carved wood, flamboyant in design and resembling the tails of dragons thrown flauntingly into the air. Of course, all the buildings of Burma save the pagoda and this wall of the fort are of teak-wood, which is almost as durable as stone.

Entering the royal enclosure by its western portal, the traveller will find himself confronted by the famous dragon throne of Burma. It is placed under the great spire of the palace, called "the centre of the world," and is really a portal in one wall of the Hall—or rather pavilion—of Audience, and is surrounded by an elaborately carved framework, all of dragon tails. Its platform is raised some three feet from the floor, and is richly ornamented by small mirrors set into its sides. Entrance to the throne

DRAGON THRONE OF KING THEEBAW, MANDALAY.

is had by means of a flight of steps in the rear, and through two sliding doors of open scrollwork, the whole, and all of the palace as well, being covered with gold-leaf which is carefully preserved around the throne, and is as brilliant to-day as when King Theebaw gazed his last from yonder doors upon his court in the hall of columns.

During the days of royalty the traveller would have been permitted to enter this throne-room, not through the great portals which stand open to-day, but through a small door so low that all must assume an humble posture as they entered the Presence. Shoes were left at that portal and were generally stolen. A squatting posture was incumbent upon all, and as this posture could not be changed it insured exquisite torture when His Majesty delayed his coming for an hour, or hours, which he often did just to impose this torture. While waiting you might observe, to the right, the hall of the Supreme Council.

All the halls of the palace are supported by columns, red at the base and gold the rest of the way, none of which are less than twenty feet in length, and as clean and solid as the day they were removed here from Amarapura.

The age of this structure does not seem to be known. Was it built new for Amarapura, or was it transported thither from some older capital? It may have made several peregrinations.

But it is hot. Let us return to the shelter of its roof. Back of the Hall of Audience are innumerable other halls used of old for the different functions of the royal establishments. The courts on both sides are occupied by the dwelling-places of those who were in attendance, and by the many tanks and towers always to be found in connection with these royal abodes.

The Upper Burman Club occupies the best preserved and the most beautiful of all the buildings, the palace of the Queen. Here is her famous lily throne, another gorgeous conception of flying dragon tails in carved wood. Its apex is a prow of a royal barge with a queen's statue as a figurehead, while other queens and princes adorn the carving up and down its sides. As with the King's throne, grilled doors give entrance from behind to a platform; it is also similar to the greater throne in being a mass of gold-leaf and mirrors. In fact, the whole structure, as well as all the walls, columns, and roof of the hall, are a mass of gold-leaf. It is truly a unique place for a club-house, and a charming place as well. The room behind the throne is a card-room, where the great American game is not neglected.

When Theebaw came into power some seventy of the blood royal were murdered within the precincts of this palace, and, it is said, were buried under the floor of this room where cards are now being played. Possibly they were claimants to the throne, and it was considered well to be quit of all chances for trouble. So the men were slaughtered, and the women also, after having been subjected to nameless tortures. " Shway Yoe " tells us that the treatment of the children recalled the days when ravaging hordes marched through the land with babes spitted on their pikestaffs for standards. The old Regent

GOLDEN PALACE OF KING THEEBAW, MANDALAY.

THE "CENTER OF THE WORLD."

of Pegu had his "nostrils and gullet plugged with gunpowder and was then blown up."

All this occurred just here while dancing and music were kept up to drown the cries of the victims. The guilt of these murders was laid at the door of the Queen and the Queen Dowager. History has repeated itself of late in the Empire of China, where the Dowager Empress holds supreme command through the medium of a weak emperor, and many executions.

But to return to the Burmese palace. The audience hall of the Queen with its stately columns is now a library and writing-room, the latter being wainscoted by screens of coloured glass, enclosing small mirrors of all shapes imaginable. In an outer room I can see punkas waving over the billiard-table, and through the vistas of the garden one may discern the summer-house where Theebaw laid down his crown at the bidding of England. The chambers of the club are in the many detached buildings of the court. Mine, from its position, must have been occupied by some favourite of the King in the old days, but to-day, if you approach any of the wooden structures, you will probably be saluted by a deep English voice demanding, "Boy, punka," or more likely a "half a peg and a split soda," but if you enter you will receive a hearty welcome, while at the same time "boy" is ordered to double up on that "peg and soda."

Life at the club at Mandalay glides smoothly and pleasantly along, and one leaves with regret and with grateful remembrances for its warm-hearted hospitality. It is full of officers of the army, and from each and all I have heard nothing save the kindest expressions of feelings towards my own land, while at the same time indignation is constantly expressed at our action in paying the Spanish a dollar for Manila. Many are the plans suggested for a closer union of our nations, one being that we furnish the army, while Great Britain furnishes the navy. Then, as one man expressed it, "The rest of the world might go to Ballyho."

After dinner last night I went to a smoking concert given in the open air and before a roaring camp-fire. All the officers of the Burma service, in full uniform, surrounded the Commanding General and the ladies of Mandalay, while on either side stretched a circle of private soldiers (English and native), and beyond them groups of grave-eyed Burmese. As for the concert, it was what might be expected from a lot of jolly soldiers, and what it lacked in artistic merit was made up in good-will and good-fellowship.

Mandalay Hill rose in the background, upon which, in ghostly array, gleamed the white pagodas of the people, while behind us clustered the temple of the seven hundred pagodas, where the religion of Buddha stands graven in stone. The usual bell-shaped structure is surrounded by more than seven hundred shrines, arranged in an immense square; in the centre of each is a tablet in stone thickly carved with portions of their holy book. The whole is enclosed by a high wall for protection, and stands a most interesting and impressive monument to the religion of Buddha.

The vicinity of Mandalay is so covered by pagodas

THE "SEVEN HUNDRED AND FIFTY PAGODAS," MANDALAY.

that it is impossible to visit many of them; but they are so much alike that when one has seen the great structure at Rangoon one has seen the best of all.

Much of Mandalay has been destroyed by fire, as wood enters largely into the construction of the city, and for months at a time there is no rain.

As the traveller passes through the streets of the city he may be pardoned if he longs for just one day's return of the court life. It would be interesting to see the King rise up from his golden throne, clothed in his robes of state and his spire-like crown, and, mounting his white elephant, proceed to the ceremony of ploughing the fields. This omitted, no good crop could be expected. White elephants, we are told, do not mean white as to colour, but simply a certain shape of the ears or a fringe on both sides of the tail. A white elephant was a sacred elephant, and could be used only by the King. Gorgeously arrayed, and shielded by a white umbrella, he sallied forth, attended by all the high dignitaries of Church and State, in crimson caps and crimson mantles, like those of a Doge in Venice.

The royal road had been shut off from the sight of his subjects by high bamboo fences through which they were not expected to peep, but through which they did peep. However, the "Rotten Row" of Burma was deserted when the King and court passed outward. He really did do a little ploughing, but spent much more time watching his fat ministers doing it. It is hot in Burma, especially in June, and the ministers did not enjoy this sacred custom, but little cared the King; he kept them at it until he grew tired of the sight, then he signalled for a return to the palace and his dragon throne, perhaps wondering the while whether some usurper had not occupied it during his absence, as often fell out in Burma. The fear of such an occurrence was one reason why a monarch rarely left the royal enclosure. If the usurper proved the stronger, the King's body passed to the keeping of the waters of the Irrawaddy, securely done up in a red velvet bag. That river has proven the sepulchre for many of the royal house.

The return to the palace was not made with that degree of splendour which marked the outgoing; the robes of state were discarded for cooler garments, and a chariot drawn by bullocks took the place of the elephant. As the cortége passed onward the city awoke to life, and the fête of the people assumed full proportions.

But fêtes and shows have passed forever from the court of the palace of Mandalay. King Theebaw lives a life of idleness and pleasure on the Bombay coast, whence but lately he sent word to the Governor of Mandalay that a new stock of wives would be acceptable, as he was tired of the thirteen who were with him.

THE "SEVEN HUNDRED AND FIFTY PAGODAS," MANDALAY.

CHAPTER IX

MONASTERIES

Foundation of the Monasteries—Queen's Golden Monastery in Mandalay—Carvings and Gildings—Sleepers and the "Butterfly Spirit"—The Enthroned Buddha and his Sanctuary—The Tower of Contemplation—Duties of a Monk—His Begging Outfit—Picturesque Costume—Closing Services before the Shrine—The Ending of the Day—Ritual of Ordination—Strange Medicines—The Four Cardinal Sins—Punishment for Violation thereof is Like that of the Leper of Old—No Supreme Being—Christianity and Buddhism Compared.

AS with God, so with Buddha, the groves are his first temples. Every monastery must be embowered in beautiful trees, for under a tree Buddha attained his full dignity. Under one he was born and died, and the last Buddha of the world will receive his office under the trees. As in the Christian faith, so in the Buddhist, kings and nobles vied with each other in erecting sacred monasteries.

The more one studies this religion, the more strongly does its resemblance to our own, in many of the lesser points, become apparent. "Take thy shoes from off thy feet" holds in Burma where these sacred buildings are concerned, for all, from the King down, must do that when they enter the holy precincts; and it is ordained by the priests that the site of every monastery is holy, as, since Buddha's time, it has been used for sacred purposes and none other. It is a pleasant sight to see the doves that congregate within these sacred enclosures; the murmuring of their cooing is music to the ear.

It is a matter of great regret that so many of the finest monasteries of Mandalay were swept away by the fire which destroyed "the incomparable pagoda." If a few more conflagrations occur there the loss to the world will be great, and that which is now a unique corner of the globe will be turned into a dusty, barren waste. As these buildings all stand detached, in separate compounds, it would seem that much that has been lost might have been saved, but, of course, being constructed of wood, the liability to blaze is great during the dry season.

Every town and hamlet of Burma possesses at least one of these sacred institutions, and in the cities they are numberless.

The Queen's golden monastery in Mandalay forms one of the most interesting collections of buildings in Burma. It is within the city and covers an entire block. The great monastery occupies the centre of the square, and around it, at a respectful distance, are placed the buildings of lesser rank, each and all beautiful in rich carving; but to describe one is to describe all, and the great building will more than suffice for that purpose. It is raised, as are all the buildings in Burma, some ten feet from the ground, the approach to this main platform being by several flights of massive steps, made of brick covered with grey cement, but all the rest of the structure is of the time-defying teak-wood.

QUEEN'S GOLDEN MONASTERY, MANDALAY.

This main platform runs entirely around the monastery, and supports three buildings of the usual Burmese form, which somewhat resembles the chalet style of architecture, save that here the lines all turn upward. Two of these buildings have lofty, many-storied, receding roofs, while the third bears on its summit a soaring, many-storied tower. Around each roof, along the ridge-poles and eaves, run standing cornices of the most delicate and elaborate carvings, while curtains of exquisite woodwork hang from the eaves. The walls of the structures are in panels with glass in the centre, and every atom is elaborately carved except the steps and the glass. All of the buildings with the exception of the high tower are covered with gold-leaf that never tarnishes. The effect, under a brilliant sunlight, and embowered in trees, can be better imagined than described.

The noonday heat has caused the monastery to be closed, and we enter through a low door in the corner, finding the place full of shadows athwart which every here and there gleam long rifts of sunlight. Gilding and red lacquer show dimly in the half-light, as does the soft, dull yellow of the silken robes of sleeping priests, or the blazing gold, brass, and bronze of the great sanctuary.

No one would dare to awaken these sleeping monks, lest the butterfly (spirit) which is off somewhere in space might be frightened and never return to its earthly habitation, and the result would mean death. This religion does not admit of a spiritual essence of any sort in man. It is considered to be merely a sixth sense called the " faculty of knowing," but it is material. They do not deny its importance, for by it a man can attain to the higher heaven through meditation which the possession of this sense enables him to carry on. But the existence of a soul and its separation from the body and flight to heaven they do not admit. However, superstition, or what you will, has crept in and proven stronger than pure doctrine, and the result is the butterfly spirit. They believe it can separate from and return to a sleeper. It is often, however, frightened away and never returns.

Dreams are to the people a sure proof of the existence of the butterfly. If two people have loved devotedly, and the death of one is followed immediately by that of the other, it is because their butterflies could not be separated. With us it would be called a broken heart. No Burman can be induced to awaken a sleeper, and so we seat ourselves in the shadow until it pleases the butterfly of some one of these yellow-robed dreamers to return to earth.

The odour of lilies is heavy on the air. The lights gleam faintly before the sanctuary where Buddha enthroned is also dreaming, his bronze features almost startled into life by one long ray of brilliant sunlight which comes slanting downward, lighting all the jewels of his crown into quivering flames. The place is a forest of shadowy golden pillars and dim recesses—a place of peace, a spot to dream in. But the butterfly spirit has returned to the abbot, who has been sleeping on a mat with a heap of yellow flowers near his head. Rousing, he welcomes us, and with dignified gestures gives us the

ENSHRINED BUDDHA GOLDEN MONASTERY, MANDALAY.

freedom of the place, and then returns to contemplation, his hands clasped around his knees, upon which his shaven head is bowed, his yellow robe flowing around him in billowy folds.

The building is of but one story, as no Burmese will allow anyone to live over him. The interior is one hall, supported by columns of red lacquer and gold, with now and then a screen between them. The colossal figure of Buddha is of brass, beautifully polished, and so perfectly joined that the lines of meeting cannot be discovered.

The many-storied tower on the right in the illustration is used as a place of retirement and meditation by the monks, in imitation of Buddha, and every passing breeze draws sweet music from its many golden bells.

The Buddhist monk is not troubled as to the spiritual welfare of his people; he has no care for the salvation of their souls. His wants are supplied by the people; if he travels they pay for it. He has simply to enter a car or steamboat, and to inform those around him that he desires to go to such and such a place. A contribution is at once taken up, his passage paid, and his food provided for. He literally takes no thought for the morrow. The people expect nothing from him in return for their charity. He is not required to preach, or to give comfort to the sick and dying, or even to assist at the last rites of the dead. In fact, all he has to do is to seek his own salvation. He must be forever poor and humble and full of kindness for man and beast. He must live apart from the world, and "observe certain moral precepts." His earthly possessions and wardrobe are scanty. He must be possessed of the *dookoht*, a yellow rectangular cloth worn in folds like a mantle; also of a cloth worn around the loins, falling to his ankles and held in place by a girdle. There is another mantle-like cloth thrown over the whole costume; he wears sandals, and his head is shaven. He carries his begging-bowl, a short-handled axe for wood-splitting, a needle, and a water-dipper. This must be a strainer, so that he runs no risk of taking animal life. A fan completes his costume.

These monks may use no colour in their dress save a dull yellow and orange, and a group of them passing in and around one of their fantastically carved temples, embowered in luxurious trees, presents a most picturesque sight.

With the dawn of day comes the clatter of the wooden gong, the *Kaladit*, making noise enough to rouse the deepest sleeper. Then comes the morning prayer: "How great a favour has the lord Buddha bestowed upon me in manifesting to me his law, through the observance of which I may escape hell and secure my salvation."

The morning service is intoned before the great image of Buddha. The simple work of the day follows—cleaning the temple, watering the sacred trees, the offering of flowers at the shrines. Meditation of some hours precedes the simple meal, which they take, not to please the appetite, but to satisfy the body.

As the sun rises and the shadows shorten, these sacred institutions assume their most picturesque appearance, for then the monks sally forth and beg their food. With their abbot at the head they descend the steps in single file, their yellow robes brought into bold relief by the grey of the foundations, while above them glitter the golden walls of the sacred house, and above all bend the magnificent trees which are always to be found surrounding them. Slowly the procession winds its way outward and into the town, and with stately steps makes its daily rounds, pausing constantly to receive the food which is showered into the alms bowl, but returning no word or glance of thanks. They confer a favour by receiving.

These alms should by the laws of Buddha furnish the daily food, but the degenerates of to-day give it to the boys, dogs, and birds, while they sit down to a well-prepared meal. In fact, the monks of to-day, with few exceptions, live very luxurious lives. They strive after the forms and ceremonies, and most of the minor things in life, but surely miss the greater end. Meditation, aside from teaching, is their principal occupation. Only by meditation does simple man become fitted for Neh'ban, and possession of the six kinds of wisdom: "the faculty of seeing like a spirit, the faculty of hearing like a spirit, creative power, knowledge of the thoughts of others, freedom from passion, knowledge of one's own past existence."

Therefore they sit and dream, and much of their dreaming is but another word for prolonged sleep.

As the sun goes down all who wear the yellow robe must be within the walls of the monastery. The scholars are examined and recite, rituals are chanted, sometimes a sermon is delivered, until the shadows deepen into night. Then the vesper lauds are chanted, after which a voice proclaims the hour, the day of the week and of the month, and the number of the year. Then the yellow-robed figures make their salutations before the abbot and before Buddha, and glide away to rest, and the day is done.

The books of the Buddhist ritual of ordination are written in characters, to read which a special education is required, and the ceremonies of consecration are too long and too elaborate to be more than referred to in a sketch like this. A candidate is examined as to his bodily health, and questioned as to any hereditary taints, as to his legitimacy, age, etc. The rule of poverty is impressed upon him, he is in duty bound to beg for food with the labour of his feet. He must gain his sustenance by his feet and not with the hands, or beg with the tongue. Buddha decreed yellow clothes made of rags from the streets, or from among tombs, but now if a monk can procure cloth or silk he may do so, and most of them do, their costumes being very rich as to texture and beautiful in colour.

The Buddhists of Burma do not dread other religions, and so long as their monastic schools are attended they have no cause for fear. All other sects are tolerated, with no apparent effect on the numbers of their following. Still, there are troubles among the faithful. There are two parties, one of which adheres strictly to the faith as Buddha gave it,—and the purest Buddhism is found here in Burma,—and the other, which has become luxurious, wears silken garments, and has made many changes.

One rule which strikes the observer as very

BUDDHIST PRIEST, MANDALAY.

strange is as follows: "It is incumbent upon an elect to use as medicine the urine of the cow or black bullock in which the juice of a lemon or other fruits has been poured." It does not say for what complaint this may prove beneficial. He is warned against four sins: carnal pleasures, stealing or coveting, killing any living thing, and the arrogation to himself of supernatural perfection or power, or to assume vainglory as a holy man. Sooner can the lofty palm that has been cut down become green again than an elect guilty of the disregard of these laws remain a member of the order. The penalty for such sin is the entire exclusion from the society, and nothing can palliate the offence. He would be stoned by the people and, in some localities, put to death. If he is excommunicated he is driven forth like a leper of old and may not drink of a running brook or a wayside fountain. He is an outcast in the fullest sense of the word. As a Mohammedan will not step on a piece of paper for fear it may contain the name of Allah, so a Buddhist must walk carefully lest he crush the smallest atom of animal life.

There is no supreme being in Buddhism; neither are there any prayers. The doxologies repeated are often the composition of the persons themselves learned at school:

"I worship the Buddha. I worship the law, etc. By worship I gain merit and purity of heart and am freed from starvation, plague, and warfare, from hell, and at last pass into Neh'ban."

This religion, while it strives for perfection in the lesser things, fails most utterly and entirely in the greater. Buddha walked forth and gave his body to save the starving tigress and her cubs. His followers are most gentle and tender of all animal life, and will not kill even a poisonous reptile in their houses, but their indifference to human life is appalling. They will not lift hand or foot to save it. How different are the teachings of the Nazarene! He gave Himself as a sacrifice, but for mankind. His doctrine teaches love and sympathy for His people. " Inasmuch as ye have done it unto one of the least of these, ye have done it unto Me" is an unknown creed among these Buddhists, but they will go out of their way to save the life of a snake. Surely the one religion is immortal, while the other will pass away when the final cycle of Buddha shall have been reached.

CHAPTER X

BURMESE CUSTOMS

Farewell to Mandalay—Brilliant Scene on the River Banks—The Women of Burma—Their Dress and Appearance—Childbirth and the Useless Suffering Enforced by "Custom"—Cargo Steamers and the Gay Life thereon—Marvellous Tattooing—Its Significance—Superstition and Magic—Horrible Customs and Weird Incantations.

NOW farewell to Mandalay. My stay here has been most interesting and delightful, and one not soon to be forgotten. I do not get off without a visit to Signior Beato's curios, and some of them will go westward with me. His display of wood-carving is especially fine. These people excel in this, and to our notion it is marvellously cheap (though the Signior does not give his curios away). Some of it is delicately beautiful, and some grotesque, but all is interesting, and being of teak-wood, it is very durable. There is also beautiful work in silver and ivory and exquisite embroideries—but it is some distance to the river and we must move on.

Travel on the Irrawaddy has lost much of its fascination since the building of the railways, still the scene on the banks as we wait to depart is full of life and interest. It is blazing hot, but that appears to make no difference, save to the Europeans, who scurry under cover. The banks are very high and very dusty. There are several steamers about to depart both up and down the river, and each has its separate crowd of travellers accompanied by the usual gang of pariah dogs that snarl and snap at every foreigner they catch sight of. Now the crowd separates and in stately procession approach a lot of yellow-robed monks, each carrying a golden umbrella, while high on the banks pass a string of elephants clanking their bells and chains and flapping their huge ears.

Yonder group of women must be persons of consequence, as they are treated with a deference fully equal to that accorded the monks. The sister of the late Queen has just died in Rangoon and these are her relatives and members of her suite going down to the funeral. That old woman in pink and blue silk is evidently of high estate, as every native man that passes her immediately kadaws * and keeps kadawing all the time he is in her presence. The entire court travel second class, notwithstanding their exalted rank.

It is marvellous that Burmese women ever consent to bear children, or rather that they should willingly run the risk of going a second time through the tortures visited upon them by the customs of the land, and " custom " in all these Eastern lands is more absolute in its power than any ruler of this world past or present.

In Burma " custom " prescribes that after a child

* See page 466, " Yoe."

BURMESE WOMAN.

is born, the poor mother, no matter what the temperature may be, shall be covered with all the rugs and blankets that can be procured. She is also heated to a burning-point by hot bricks placed under her body. This is kept up for a week, when what is left of the poor creature, who is generally a mere child, is allowed to go free; but years have been added to her appearance, so that an old hag has been produced from what was but a month back a fresh young girl.

There is not a young face among all that gaily dressed group, and most of them are wizened and old as a woman should not be at sixty. When gotten up *en fête*, however, these Burman women present a gay appearance. The costumes are always composed of soft silk, which lends itself to graceful draping. Yonder stands one with a pink silk sarong, which falls from the waist quite to her feet in graceful folds, very unlike the stiff, immodest fashion prevalent with that garment in Java. She wears a white waist, and a pale yellow scarf. Her masses of black hair are coiled on the top of her head with a bunch of flowers inserted just over the ear. You can easily see that aside from a pair of sandals she wears no other clothing. She certainly looks clean, yet, judging from the many strange scenes connected with the toilet, which one witnesses in the street, the appearance may be deceptive.

The costume of the men is apparently exactly the same as that of the women save for a slight shortening of the sarong. There are dozens of these gaily dressed individuals on the river bank, watching our departure, and the scene is a brilliant one. Our route is down-stream and we have taken passage on a cargo boat, one of those curious craft which supply the river people with all they desire, and which afford an opportunity to study Burmese life to excellent advantage.

To either side of a paddle steamer is attached a double-decked barge, and thereon are to be found almost all the articles that Edgeware Road or Sixth Avenue can produce, very few native goods being displayed. Halts are made at every village and the people swarm on board by the hundreds, and great is the haggling, noise, and confusion. It is curious to watch the manner in which this is kept up over every article purchased, until the last warning whistle drives the crowds ashore.

The shrewdness of the women is observed to best advantage upon these boats where hundreds of them pass most of their lives selling their wares. They are more than a match for any of the men-folks, and woe be to the thief who hopes to profit by the confusion. He will not get far away if he gets even a start, which is doubtful.

It is reported that foreigners who have formed relations with the women of Burma have found them very faithful in all respects, but they are vengeful and unforgiving, and rumour hath it that several English brides who have come out here have been done away with through the medium of powdered glass or drugs. An order was lately issued to the men in the Civil Service that they must end all relations with these women, but several preferred to marry them, and did so. One man living in the outer wilderness could procure no minister or magistrate to perform the ceremony for him, nor could he obtain leave of absence in order to go to some town. Therefore being a magistrate himself he promptly tied the knot between himself and the dame. This was held by the local authorities to be illegal, but he carried his case to Parliament, and coming off triumphant, now lives in tropical bliss, with elephants, tigers, and snakes as his nearest neighbours.

The natives are a kindly people and their religion teaches them to be so. It is considered most meritorious to save animal life. One of our passengers, having caught two large catfish which no one would eat, was asked by a Burmese if they could be bought, and they were sold to him for something like fifty cents, their purchaser immediately restoring them to their native element. When a poor native will spend what to him is a large sum for such a purpose it means much.

On a bamboo raft close by, a lot of boys are sporting and working, and like boys of other countries there is more sport than work on hand just at present. A stranger at first glance will pay no attention to them, as there seems nothing worthy of remark, but a second glance is followed by a third, and then the field-glass comes into requisition for a closer inspection. The boys appear to be naked, save for a pair of grey knickerbockers or knee-breeches, but the knickerbockers prove to be, in reality, a mass of tattooing.

In Japan, tattooing is considered now as an ornament, but with the Burmese boy it is held to be quite as necessary as his monastic instructions, and without it he does not consider that he has attained full manhood, and one who omits the operation is looked upon as almost unsexed and altogether beneath contempt. Therefore every boy undergoes the painful operation, which, when completed, puts him in possession of a mass of dark blue traceries extending from the waist-line to below the knee cap. If you are desirous of being so adorned the artist will come to you with his tools and patterns from which you make a selection. The figures of cats, tigers, and elephants, and also many mythological designs, are used, and each is surrounded by an oval frame of tracing, and sometimes by a variety of alphabetical letters. These designs are artistically traced upon the person and the interspaces filled by a delicate lace-like tracery. The waist and knee-lines are distinctly marked and have the appearance of girdle and garter. Often the most important designs are done in scarlet, which when the operation is finished stand forth in a startling fashion upon the dark blue background of the rest of the work.

The operation is painful, and can only be done by degrees, opium being often used upon the subject to deaden the pain. The blue dye comes from lampblack and never disappears, but the red fades gradually. The " drug of tenderness " is a mixture of vermilion with a variety of herbs and other things, one of these ingredients being the bruised and dried skin of the spotted lizard, the mascot of the Burmese home. Superstition states that a tattoo of this magic fluid will enable a youth to gain the maiden of his choice, and it is always placed in a

TATOOED BOY.

small design between the eyes. This is the only form of tattooing ever used by women, but they place it where it cannot be seen. "Yoe" tells us that in Rangoon the tattooing of a woman means that she desires an Englishman for a husband, and then he adds "poor thing."

The legends and superstitions connected with this tattooing are without number, running from the commonplace to the most weird and fantastic. The "a-kyan say" is the most gruesome of the list, and few tattooers "are acquainted with the necessary drugs and incantations." Great courage is necessary, and many men have lost their minds while undergoing the operation, and have taken to graveyard wanderings and digging for human bones. "Yoe" states that this is not to be wondered at, as, during the operation, the tattooers make them chew the raw flesh of a man who has been hanged. The charm seems to be produced by the use of singular drugs and weird incantations. The results are various: sometimes a man becomes possessed of marvellous strength; sometimes he can walk on the water or sink into the ground; often he becomes a dacoit and is restored to his right mind only by sacred drugs and by the removal of the fatal figure. Many believe that certain figures will prevent drowning. This experiment was tried in Rangoon, where a boy that had been so tattooed requested to be tied hand and foot and thrown into the river, fully believing that he would be saved from the swift current. But the Irrawaddy, so near its union with the ocean, carried him away forever. No such tragedy will occur amongst those boys yonder, for they cling tightly to the raft as it rises and falls on the waves made by the wheels of our departing steamboat. A bend in the shore shuts them and the gay crowd on the banks from view, and Mandalay vanishes from my sight.

CHAPTER XI

ANCIENT PAGAHN

Pagodas Crowd the Banks of the Irrawaddy—Meaning of the Word " Pagoda "—The " Kyaik-htee-yoh "—Its Fantastic Position and Legends—Pagahn—A City Dead Seven Hundred Years—Its Foundations — Destruction — Countless Pagodas — Present State—The Anada Pagoda—The Majestic Appearance of the Buddha—The Solemn Expression of its Face and the Meaning thereof—" A Face from out Nirvana, where no Fear is "—Size of the Anada—Its Four Sanctuaries—Pagoda Slaves, their Service and Outcast Position — Tradition of their Origin — Treachery of Pagahn's King—Petty State of the Slaves—The Vision of Vanishing Pagahn—The Silence of the River.

MANDALAY is the heart of Burma. On its outskirts stood the old capital of Amarapura, to-day but a mass of pagodas, and as the traveller approaches the point where the river is crossed by the railroad ferry the prospect becomes fairly bewildering. On every hilltop, in every gully, in all the valleys, and down even into the waters of the river, stand the sacred structures, a vast city of them. An illustration of Mandalay, in the *London News* of November 26th, gives a view of the "four hundred and fifty pagodas surrounding the ' Aracan,' " whereas the Aracan Pagoda, which is the great shrine of Mandalay, is some miles away from the " four hundred and fifty " on the other side of the town. I have not described the Aracan for the reason that it has been partly destroyed by fire and is in a state of great confusion, and because a description of too many pagodas becomes wearisome, and we have yet to visit many, including that marvel of the world, the " Shway Dagohn " at Rangoon.

The word " Buddha " signifies " enlightened," while the word "pagoda" means "relic shrine," and should only be used for such buildings as contain some relic of Buddha. Here again is a resemblance between the treasure chambers of a pagoda and the corner-stone of a Christian church: the one holds its relics and jewels, the other its books and records.

Buddha left no instructions in regard to pagodas, but desired that a small mound, steep like a heap of rice, should be raised over his bones. The original shrines which held the relics were shaped like the lotus bulb, and the present bell-shaped structure seems an elaboration of this. The Buddha in the womb of Queen Maia resembled a lotus bulb.

A source of great surprise to the traveller is the marvellous and apparently inaccessible position in which some of these pagodas are placed; and quite the most remarkable in this respect is that of " Kyaik-htee-yoh " in the Moulmein district. Upon the summit of a hill thirty-five hundred feet high, and upon the very apex of a balancing boulder, which in turn rests upon a projecting rock, is perched this small pagoda. The chasm which separates the peak from the nearest hill is said to reach far below the surface of the earth. The boulder appears to rock with every passing wind, and one cannot but

"KYAIK-HTEE-YOH" PAGODA, MOULMEIN.

wonder why it does not disappear, pagoda and all, into the gulf surrounding it. During the winter months the people come in crowds to this shrine, and, after casting jewels and money into the chasm, clamber up to the rocks and decorate the pagoda with flowers and candles. The little structure has been there longer than history can tell. Some give its age as more than five thousand years. The faithful will tell you that this boulder is kept in place by a hair of the great Buddha, given to a hermit by the saint himself on "his return from the second heaven of the 'Nat-dewah's,' where he had been proclaiming the law to his mother." Near this pagoda is a spring, which ceases to flow if evil talk is indulged in, or if the sexes are not separated.

The shrines and pagodas of the Irrawaddy multiply more and more as we proceed southward, until it is almost impossible to believe that no life exists amidst what appears to be a vast city. But, listen as you will, the silence is unbroken save by the splash of the boat's paddles and the murmur of the river. The scene is dreamlike, and the heart of dreamland is reached as we near the long-dead city of Pagahn.

The ancient name of Burma was "Mien" and Pagahn was its capital. Marco Polo was dead in 1325, yet what he describes of the city was very ancient at that period. It was in the year of Christ 1272 that the army of the Great Khan came down upon Pagahn, and the Prince of "Mien" went forth to give him battle. In the midst of the latter's army stalked two thousand elephants, each carrying its tower of timbers. There were sixteen armed warriors in every tower. Of horsemen and foot-soldiers there were sixty thousand. With this mighty host he moved forward to where the captain of the Tartar army awaited him. But the "battle is not to the strong alone." The forces of the Khan amounted to but twelve thousand well-mounted men. At first, their horses took such fright at the sight of the elephants and their wonderful burdens that the riders could not control them, and they turned and fled, but the commander ordered his men to dismount and tie the animals to trees. The riders were thus enabled to use their bows and arrows to such good effect that the elephants of the pagan host, maddened by the shafts, fled in the wildest terror, trampling hundreds of that army to death, and sweeping off the towers on their own backs against the trees. So great was the press of fleeing men and beasts that numbers of the former were suffocated, and the din of battle was as the thunder. The rout was complete and the conqueror swept on towards Pagahn.

The vision presented by the capital was wonderful to their eyes. From the midst of the vast city, with its countless houses, endless avenues of shrines, stately temples, and majestic statues of Buddha, rose two vast towers, which Marco Polo describes as being, "the one of gold, the other of silver, the precious metals being laid upon the stone, of which the towers were built, to the depth of a finger." Each tower was "ten paces in height, and of breadth in proportion," the upper parts were "round, and girt with gold and silver bells, which tinkled as the wind blew." There was a tomb between the towers plated with gold and silver. These towers and the tomb were erected by a former king to commemorate his own magnificence and for the good of his soul. "They form one of the sights of the world, and shine forth resplendent, as the sun's rays strike them." The tales of all their glory being carried to the court of the Great Khan, he commanded that they be left untouched, as "no Tartar will lay hands on anything appertaining to the dead." History is silent as to when they were finally destroyed, or by whom. Probably the hand of unmolested time has been the culprit, but we may behold the equal of either, if not their superior, in the Great Pagoda of Rangoon.

It is seven hundred years since Pagahn ceased to live. Very long and valiant was its defence. Six thousand temples were pulled down to build its forts, but without avail. The city fell and remains a ruin, silent and deserted to this day. The foundation of Pagahn is placed by some as long ago as A.D. 52, when the people from Prome, far down the river, came and settled here, and the religion of Buddha lived and flourished. Pagahn was the centre of the busy life of ancient Burma until the day when the hordes of China descended the river and swept it out of existence.

Travellers to-day will land at a small place up the river, and must be prepared to take care of themselves, for strangers are not provided for in any way in this city of the dead, which stretches eight miles along the river, and four miles inland. Save for the few wretched huts of the people who care for the more sacred shrines, there is no sign of life amid all this chaos and ruin. An ancient gateway receives us in melancholy fashion; there are no guards, no banners, no sound save the slight rustle of a snake disturbed in its noonday slumbers. Passing onward, the appalling desolation of the old city comes fully into view, as avenue after avenue stretches away on either side, and the long vista in front shows nothing save ruins. The hand of the passing centuries has fallen heavily upon Pagahn, sparing nothing save a few temples that the pious have kept in repair, and foremost among these is the great shrine, the Anada Pagoda, which rises more like a Christian cathedral than a Buddhist temple.

Two gigantic leogryphs guard the approach to the arched entrance, and one passes under the solemn arches and through the welcome shadows of the old temple, and, in passing, notes the many cross walks and intersecting courts, but is attracted to the centre of the structure, where, by some arrangements of the lights from far above, the great god stands forth and seems to beckon the pilgrim even as he enters the first portal; as he approaches the sanctuary he will fall upon his knees if he be of the faith, and if a Christian, his hat will come off his head in very reverence for this majesty before him. All is in shadow, save the Buddha himself, upon whom descends the glory of light.

Unlike most other statues of the god, this is standing and is some forty feet in height. One hand is extended as though in invitation or benediction; the face is solemn, grave, and peaceful, a face from out Nirvana, where no fear is entertained of further weary and endless reincarnations, while

RUINED PAGAHN, ANADA PAGODA IN DISTANCE.

upon it rests the calm, eternal, sleep-like smile. Here one seems to understand the expression of all those faces which have puzzled one for so long. It means the attainment of Nirvana, the end of the cycles of transincorporation of souls, the death of all human passions and feeling; means that the hopes and fears of life no longer have part or place; means peace, after all. Is not that a more correct or acceptable idea than many that are set forth in our churches, which give no idea of rest or peace ? and what can heaven be without those attributes ?

The solemn silence that hangs over this spot, the absence of human life and sound, adds wonderfully to the impressiveness of this great shrine of Pagahn, and it is with difficulty that one can turn from it for a closer inspection of the temple itself. The Anada, nearly three hundred feet in length and breadth, is in plan a large square with four projecting sections, and the whole, save at the very centre, is intersected by numerous corridors and passages which cross each other at right angles. There are four main entrances which proceed straight to four shrines, situated on each side of the inner square. This square is nearly a solid block, supporting the great spire or dome, and the sanctuaries are niches in each side, wherein stands in each one a colossal statue such as I have described. They are of the four great Buddhas of this world cycle. In the east "Kauk-Kathan," the first lawgiver, made of the dan-ta-goo tree; "Gawnagohng" in the southern chamber is of jasmine wood; Kathapa in the western niche is of brass; while the Gautama Buddha in the northern is of fir, and is the one I have described. They have all been covered with plaster, and all are gilded, but their age is unknown, though it is very great.

There are other sacred shrines in Pagahn, but the one of Anada is the most sacred and the most interesting, so I shall not describe any of the others.

But let us mount and gaze outward on the city itself. What a picture of silence, desolation, and decay! What a mass of ruins the 9999 pagodas present! Verily it was a sacred city, for, to-day, save a fragment of the fort, a gate, and a bit of wall, nothing remains except these sacred structures, the number of which in Pagahn, even in her ruin, makes the eye tired, the brain weary, and the heart sad.

These Buddhists lay no claim for a divine origin for Buddha. They praise and strive to emulate him as a perfect man, but as a man, not a god, and as one that has ceased to exist, and possesses now no power of any sort. The idolatry among them is only with the very ignorant. The images of Buddha simply represent an idea. But one can easily understand how these simple-minded people can actually bow down and worship yonder stately Buddha, whose majestic, awe-inspiring face is even now illumined with the glory of the sun.

A remarkable statue of Buddha is to be found in a pagoda near the foot of Mandalay Hill—remarkable from its size, and because it is a monolith. It is in the usual sitting posture and is twenty-five feet high, and of course its weight is enormous. In the olden days a great ruby gleamed from its marble forehead. In the large enclosure around it are rows

GREAT STATUE OF BUDDHA, ANADA PAGODA, PAGAHN.

of small shrines, each holding its sitting Buddha and all facing the central shrine. If the Buddha is made of brass, the casting of the figure is the occasion of a great festival. When completed it is carried in procession, attended by music and dancing, to the shrine prepared for its reception. The highest in the land assist at these functions and consider themselves honoured in so doing; but if honoured at their creation, little reverence is shown to-day, save with few exceptions, to the thousands of sad-eyed Buddhas that gaze outward from the ruined fanes of Pagahn.

Before the British took possession of Burma each pagoda had its slaves,—those who kept it clean,—and they were slaves in every sense of the word. No human power could free them, and throughout all time they and their descendants must so remain until the cycle of Gauṭama's religion shall have passed away. They were outcasts and despised by all, nor could they be employed in any other capacity than the one mentioned. Upon being freed they were obliged to disguise their identity and hide their past before any work could be procured. Why it should be so has not been explained. This service was not disgusting, nor any more degrading than that of a sexton in England, yet they were outcasts like the mummifiers in Egypt, and disputed their food with the pariah dogs and crows, quarrelling and fighting over the rice offered up at the shrine. The vendors of flowers and candles are all of this class. Here in Pagahn they are thicker than elsewhere and assume a royal dignity like the beggars in "Notre Dame." They have a king, who goes forth under a golden umbrella, but from whom the lowest in Burma would shrink with loathing.

Tradition states that this strange sect had its origin centuries ago when a king of Pagahn, suspecting the loyalty of a tributary sovereign, "invited him to the great and noble city with its towers of gold and silver, of which Marco Polo writes." The monarch came without fear and but scantily attended. Then, during a great feast, when all were assembled at the pagoda of Shway-zee-gohn, he was seized by the hair and a sword waved over his head, thus dedicating him and all his followers and their descendants throughout all time to the service of the great shrine. Hence this petty state before us, all the semblance of royal life in Pagahn to-day. Why they continue to exist is a marvel, but they do, and increase and multiply, marrying amongst themselves.

The Irrawaddy widens into a lake below Pagahn, and as we pass to the lower bank the ancient city takes on an unearthly beauty. Towers and temples are once more of gold and silver. White pagodas, forts, walls, minarets, and palm trees float mirage-like, until one wonders if that is not the vision which has tormented so many weary pilgrims in far-off deserts. Now it is illumined with a pale pink glow, and, like the city of Aladdin, has separated from the earth and is floating outward and upward until it gradually fades and fades and disappears, leaving nothing save the lake-like glimmering river below, while above one great sparkling planet hangs in the high heavens against the dark blue sky into which Pagahn has vanished forever. Then the murmuring river carries us onward into the silence of the night.

CHAPTER XII

RANGOON

The "Shway Dagohn Payah"—First Appearance from the Sea—Its Fascination for the Traveller—Its Age and Unaltered State—Regilding and the Cost—The Sacred Stairs and the Dwellers thereon—The Marvellous Appearance of the Great Platform—Majestic Appearance of the Great Pagoda—Its Jewelled Umbrella and Golden Bells—Lilies and Lotus—The Legend of the Scarlet Canna—Last Appearance of the Sacred Stairs and Grinning Leogryphs.

ON the last spur of the Pegu Hills, advancing far out into the valley of Rangoon, stands the "Shway Dagohn Payah," the most sacred and most remarkable shrine in all the Buddhist world—sacred because it is the only "Payah" known to the Buddhists which contains not only the sacred hair of Shin Gautama, but relics (a drinking-cup, a robe, and a staff) of the three Buddhas who preceded him. Therefore to this spot come countless pilgrims from every quarter of the world to which this faith has penetrated. The hill upon which the structure stands has been cut into two rectangular terraces which rise to a height of one hundred and sixty-six feet above the level of Rangoon, the upper terraces forming a square seven hundred by nine hundred feet, and from this for three hundred and seventy feet soars the great golden bell, so that its summit reaches a height, above the city, almost equal to that of the Washington Monument.

To the traveller approaching from the sea the pagoda is a vision of dazzling brilliancy and is visible long before the low-lying shores and distant mountains have evolved themselves from the waste of waters. If the approach is in the early morning when the sun has not yet risen his eyes will gaze into a misty void, grey and colourless, but with the first rays of approaching light a vision as of something celestial will be sharply silhouetted against the darkness, something which has fallen from the walls of heaven, and now floats a golden glory for the delight and astonishment of man. As the light increases this brilliancy becomes almost too dazzling for mortals to gaze upon. Finally the mists grow thinner and thinner, and then sail away, leaving the structure resting upon a mound of delicate green that rolls downward and away across the valley where stands the city of Rangoon, and where the Irrawaddy forces its way to the ocean.

The traveller will find that the fascination of this first glimpse has been so great, and has so aroused his curiosity, that he will pass the city by unnoticed and press onward eagerly for a closer inspection of the shrine. Of its age there is no authentic record. Buddhists place the date of its erection 588 B.C., but "Yoe" thinks the site must have been sacred for cycles before that, as the relics of the three preceding Buddhas were found interred on the spot; at least we have the certainty that we see it now substantially as it stood five hundred years before our

ENTRANCE TO SHWAY DAGOHN PAGODA, RANGOON.

religion came into existence. It is so sacred that it is kept in perfect condition, and twice within the last century it has been completely regilded. Sinbyoo Shin, a king who lived one hundred years ago, spent £9000 in the work, and this was repeated by King Mindohn in 1871.

As the traveller approaches the hill he will be confronted by two colossal leogryphs in stone and plaster, strangely grinning beasts that guard nearly all these great pagodas. There is a legend connected with these grotesque figures, a pathetic and touching story, which goes to show that in all religions, amidst all peoples, a mother and a mother's love are reverenced as scarcely less than divine.

These leogryphs represent a lion which in the old days, rescued and suckled a king's son who had been abandoned. Upon reaching manhood he fled from his strange mother and swam a river to escape her. Upon his desertion her heart broke and she died, and so in memory of her devotion and love these figures guard the entrance to all that is most holy amongst the Buddhists.

Behind the leogryphs rises an elaborate arch in stone, the entrance to a holy staircase leading direct to the great platform of the pagoda, far above on its terrace. This staircase, covered its entire length by an arching roof, is ornamented every here and there with carvings which would do justice to Gibbons. Its shallow steps force one to ascend slowly, and they are so slippery that one is tempted for safety's sake to assume the devotional attitude incumbent upon the devotees at the "Scala Santa" in Rome.

On either side the people display their wares, which are mostly such as may be offered up at some shrine in the temple. Each sets forth the caste and nationality of the owner. Here are Chinese toys and coloured tapers of strange shapes.

Each day has an animal as a symbol, and these red and yellow wax candles are modelled thereafter, and then offered at the shrines. Monday has a tiger, Tuesday a lion, Wednesday an elephant, Thursday a rat, Friday a guinea-pig, Saturday a dragon, and Sunday a half-beast, half-bird, which is supposed to guard the centre of the universe. Yonder is the silk of the Burmese, and everywhere are paper banners. But most of all one sees those yellow and red lilies so loved of the Buddha, and there are also great trays of purple and pink lotus blossoms.

As the summit is reached, and one steps on to the great platform of the pagoda, one must be dumb indeed not to be struck with amazement at the sight presented. Imagine a vast enclosure, adorned by stately trees, and surrounded by a wall, breast high, beyond which one catches glimpses of misty plains, distant mountains, and sparkling ocean. Countless shrines of all sizes and descriptions stand in regular aisles around the enclosure. Under the canopy of each sits a figure of Buddha, and sometimes a whole court of Buddhas, some of gold, many of stone, old and grey, while others are of carved wood. Each and all, however, keep their distance, allowing a broad sweep of empty promenade between their lesser splendour and the glory of the great pagoda, which from the centre of the plaza soars high aloft,

THE "SHWAY DAGOHN," RANGOON.

higher than the dome of St. Paul's, a mass of glittering gold, made more brilliant, more magnificent, by the light of the setting sun. Its base is a square with receding terraces, while its graceful bell-shaped lines ascend until they terminate in a sacred "T," or umbrella, whose surface is encrusted with jewels, and from whose lace-like fringe many tinkling bells send down sweet music with each passing breeze.

In the centre of each side of the base of the pagoda stands an elaborate pavilion of teak-wood, its columns encrusted with coloured glass, while every gable, angle, and corner is rich with delicate wood-carvings, black with age. The usual flaring dragons' tails deck the summit of the receding stories of these pavilions, and under them sit the most sacred Buddhas, before which crouch murmuring groups of priests, robed in yellow. Countless tapers gleam in the inner shadows, yellow and red flowers are cast broadcast at the feet of the saint, and the faint scent of the lotus pervades the air. Around the first terrace of the great pagoda are rows of squatting stone elephants, and vases used to receive the offerings of the people, while on the top of this terrace stands a row of small pagodas, but above them nothing mars the upward-sweeping lines of the great structure, glistening against a fair blue sky.

The effect is most majestic and imposing. It is said that the jewels flashing on the umbrella represent a sum of £50,000 sterling, all voluntary subscriptions from these simple-looking people, headed by their king. Many of the smaller pagodas are the same shape as the great one, many are Chinese in design, but each and all keep their distance from the central structure, and all the worshippers in all the shrines face its glittering surface.

In one pagoda near me kneels a picturesque group of priests, clothed in yellow silk, and holding aloft bunches of red and yellow lilies, while they keep up a monotonous chant to the music of a sweet-sounding gong. Here and there stand tall poles which bear on high winged figures, and whose bases are guarded by grotesque figures of men and animals.

One of the side temples holds no less than seventeen figures of Buddha, some colossal, some small, all seated in the unvarying fashion always found in Burma—cross-legged, with the soles of the feet turned upward, the palm of one hand in a like position, while the other hand hangs over the knee. The garments of the figures are gilded, but the flesh is white, and each wears a sacred cap.

In the centre of this shrine, under a glass case, is a life-size, reclining figure in alabaster of Buddha in the position in which he died. It is adorned with many fine gems in cap and girdle, and rests on a golden couch, while before it quantities of lilies and purple lotus have been scattered by the faithful.

But the favourite flower is the scarlet canna, so common at home, which these people believe to have sprung from the blood of Buddha when his brother-in-law attempted to destroy him by means of a huge rolling stone. The boulder burst, and a fragment only touched the toe of Shin Gautama, drawing a few drops of blood, from whence sprang the scarlet flower.

This great shrine at Rangoon is not the work of a

COURT OF THE DYING BUDDHA, RANGOON.

day, but, as each month passes, some pagoda is added, and this will be done until there is room for no more—a date not far distant.

But the shadows lengthen and the faithful have departed, leaving me alone but for the yellow-robed figure of one priest boy, who kneels close by me, holding between his clasped hands a crimson lily, while his murmured incantations mingle with the music of countless wind-swept bells.

The holy staircase is deep in shadows, save where the sunlight illumines the dying flowers. I pass downward over heaps of the lotus, and my hands are crimson from the lilies which I gather. There is no soul visible in all the darkening vista but some few blind beggars whose sun set long ago. How pure Buddha intended his faith to be! How far from pure it is to-day! How are his people fallen! The leogryphs at the entrance of his greatest shrine seem to smile at the sarcasm of destiny as the sun goes down.

CHAPTER XIII

EN ROUTE TO MANILA

Departure from Rangoon—News of the German Emperor—French, Germans, and English in the East—Feelings of an American on their Ships—Actions of the Germans there—Their Relations to America and their Sympathy for Spain—German Designs on Manila—General Lack of a Proper Understanding as to the Cause of our "Little War"—Spain's Refusal to Clean Havana—Position of our Government as Regards the *Maine*—The Cubans and Mexicans—Effect of our "Little War"—Union of our People—Position of England—Intelligent Understanding of our "Jingoes"—Our Histories—Our Congressmen—Wars of a Century ago Relegated to their Niche in History—Salute of our Flag at Manila by the English.

AS we leave Burma word comes that the German Emperor has had a broad smooth road made for him to the Garden of Gethsemane. If I remember aright, both His Royal Highness the Prince of Wales and General Grant were ushered into Jerusalem by bands of music, but, of all places on earth, should not that old Judæan fortress, that shrine and that tomb, be the spots where all remembrance of human greatness should shrink away and be as nothing? Surely to have a smooth road made for any mortal to the Garden of Gethsemane is almost a sacrilege—to that spot, of all others, let mortal man

ENSHRINED GAUTAMAS SURROUNDING THE SHWAY DAGOHN PAGODA, RANGOON.

approach on bended knee, and in the silence of the night, for those old, gnarled olive trees that witnessed the Passion of Jesus of Nazareth are full of His presence to this day, and the heart must be hard indeed that does not desire to "go apart and pray yet a little while."

News comes also of the fall of Khartoum and the avenging of Gordon. Again the nineteenth century has triumphed over the eighth, and with the passing of the power of Spain and that of the Mahdi, the Dark Ages recede more and more into the background of history.

The face of the Sirdar is strong and most interesting to contemplate. He has written a page of the world's story. This conflict in the Soudan will be followed by the building of the railroad from the Cape to Cairo, and where the railway enters progress and civilisation attain a sure footing. The fall of Khartoum and the fall of Manila will afford the world an opportunity of passing sentence upon the difference in the recognition of service accorded by a monarchy and a republic.

In this journey toward Manila we have travelled on German, French, and English ships. The Frenchmen have always been courteous and polite. If they object, which should not surprise us, to our conquest over their cousins of the Latin race they do not show it, yet they have vast commercial connections and strong blood ties with Spain, and they are of the same religion. The same holds true with Italy and Austria. We have felt at home on the English ships—no more need be said. But on the German ships and with the German merchants, from first to last, there has been an aggressive, hostile feeling—and why? Certainly nothing in the past century has more surprised and wounded the feelings of America than the knowledge of this feeling. Our sympathies were strongly with Germany in the Franco-Prussian war. That nation has the closest blood ties with quite one-third of our millions of people; her trade interests with us are enormous; her freedom of religion is the same; and she claims to have all the advanced ideas, manners, and customs of the Anglo-Saxon. Yet out here she has shown and is still showing the strongest sympathy with the old rotten monarchy of Spain, a nation with whose people she holds not one thing in common. The Germans may deny that they have any "hostile feeling" against us, yet the fact remains that wherever they are met with on this side of the world they are most bitter. (I regret to make this statement, as my blood is strongly German.) After giving utterance to such bitterness, they will turn and recount incidents of Spanish vileness, dirt, filth, robbery, outrage, and murder, and, when asked how they can have any sympathy with such a people, they cannot answer.

It is impossible to believe that any German, from the Emperor down, can really desire to alienate his nation from America, but these actions in the East have certainly done the Fatherland an injury, for I believe that the millions of Germans in America—the land that has received and protected them and their families, where they have made their fortunes and held their homes in perfect peace and freedom—would side with the land of their adoption in case

WOOD CARVINGS, SHWAY DAGOHN PAGODA, RANGOON.

of real trouble. That the Germans care for Spaniards as Spaniards one cannot for an instant imagine, but that they wanted those islands for themselves would appear to be beyond a doubt. Whether they intended to appropriate or buy them from worn-out, bankrupt Spain they alone know, but they fully intended to obtain them. How great was their rage, therefore, to have the entire plan thwarted by America in one single May morning! Had Admiral Von Diederichs succeeded in his attempt at that time, his Government would not have disowned his actions. "Nothing succeeds like success!"

There seems to be a strange lack of knowledge even among some of the English out here as to the true cause of our late war. They appear to know of none save the destruction of the *Maine*. All the years of irritation since the *Virginius* affair one would judge are forgotten. The constant petty insults, the awful loss of life by yellow fever year after year through the existence of that cesspool—Havana—just at our door, the millions of money spent in quarantine because Spain refused to take any sanitary measures whereby thousands of lives in our land might have been saved,* the horrible murders, robberies, and outrages in these islands, not only upon the Cubans, but upon many of our own people—all seem forgotten, only the wholesale slaughter of our men on the *Maine* being remembered. It is not to be supposed that the Spanish Government was directly concerned in that destruction, but she knew the dangers of the buoy at which she deliberately placed our ship,—an action which was thoroughly

* Under our rule July 1st finds no yellow fever in Havana.

Spanish,—therefore she was in every way responsible for what occurred. She had nothing to gain by the destruction of the *Maine*, and everything to lose. That she was betrayed—as she has been so many times, as Ireland and Poland always were—by some of her subjects, for personal spite, or by sale to the Cubans, is very probable. The Cubans would have moved heaven and earth to accomplish such a disaster, and the destruction of hundreds of our men would not have deterred them for an instant. They are half-breeds, and possess all the vices of the mother-country, and none of her virtues.

A like population exists in Mexico, where nothing but the strong hand of Dictator Diaz has redeemed that land from the reign of murder and robbery which prevailed when I first visited it in 1879, when it was not safe to walk the streets of the City of Mexico in the early twilight. Neither could one walk alone in the morning down her Paseo to Chapultepec. Even as late as 1888, trains from the north were fired into as they passed along. Diaz's orders were " prompt execution if caught," and many of the miscreants were caught. There, as in Manila, an ignorant, grasping priesthood was largely responsible for such a state of affairs. The priests knew that with the advent of enlightenment from the north their power would end, and it has ended. However, it may be that a Higher Power has directed this so-called " little war." It may be that an end of the old Spanish Empire was intended, and that to the young Republic was allotted the task. At all events, the " little war " has been productive of great results. It has shown to the world what Europe did not believe—the perfect union of our people. Our family quarrel was our own quarrel, and when a foreign foe came up our boys promptly marched from all sections of the land, and, standing shoulder to shoulder, went forth to meet its foes as they will ever go. There was no North, South, East, or West, but all were as one, and had the President required millions of men he would have had no difficulty in securing them.

The second great achievement was the showing to the world, and to our "jingoes" at home, the true sentiments of Great Britain. To the thinker or the traveller these sentiments have of late years been very evident, but our land is full of men who never travel—many of whom have been sent to Congress. There they have not hesitated to blare forth their supposed knowledge of the present conditions of the nations of the earth, especially of England, all of which knowledge has been learned from our school histories, books which had better be promptly remodelled and brought up to date, especially the histories studied years since by the men now in Congress, and which deal almost entirely with the old wars of a century ago and more. Year after year Concord has been fought again, Ticonderoga taken, Yorktown reviewed. All the time has been spent in this schoolboy gloating over this past—rarely is the present or future studied at all. There should be a law in America making travel and a proper appreciation of the world and its people requisites for election to offices where such appreciation and knowledge are absolutely necessary. If any man with such knowledge will go to the halls of Congress, he will come away scarcely proud of many of the members of that body. Our history is a glorious one, and all Americans are, justly, proud of it; but give it its niche in the past, study it forever, but also know the present, and live in the age in which you are born. Of the work Great Britain has done, and is doing the world over, most Americans have known and cared just nothing at all, but have lived under the firm conviction that England, since she lost us, has had her guns ever trained westward to retake Bunker Hill.

That our occupation of the Philippines has been greatly to the taste of that empire is very evident. We are the one nation on the globe that she would willingly see in possession. It may be claimed that her actions are all based upon self-interest. True, very likely, as she is human, and as self-interest has been at the base of most actions since the days when the serpent tempted Mother Eve.

When Her Majesty the Queen goes to her rest she will be sincerely mourned in America. We still remember that, when the clouds lowered darkest in our own land, the Queen and the late Prince Consort were ever our friends, and to them alone we owe a great debt of gratitude for being spared an awful war with England. The note which Lord Palmerston prepared for us on the Mason and Slidell matter was one that no self-respecting nation could have accepted. It meant war, but fortunately it passed into the hands of Prince Albert, who remodelled its contents, and, when signed by Her Majesty, it became a missive of peace.

After all, little things make up the sum of this

life, and when the English fleet, by the notes of the *Star-Spangled Banner*, saluted the ships of Admiral Dewey as they steamed into battle, it knocked on the hearts of our people. For that action, and for saluting our flag as it was raised over Manila, the German Admiral censured the Englishman, telling him that his Government "would not approve." How greatly it disapproved is shown by the increased honours bestowed upon him.

At Singapore we find the *Raleigh* homeward bound for a deserved rest. I have the pleasure of meeting her officers upon several occasions, and, for the first time, hear the true reports concerning the actions of Admiral Von Diederichs; but the story will undoubtedly be told upon the arrival of the *Raleigh* at New York, if our Government so desires it. Certainly it would not be proper to insert it here.

CHAPTER XIV

MANILA

The Stormy China Sea—Communication with the Islands—First Appearance of the City—Landing—Hotels—A Devotee at the Shrine of *Mañana* Forced to Deal with a Nation of "To-day" —The Result—The American Accent and Language in the Far East—First Walks through the City—The Rush in the Streets—The Strange Vehicles—The English Hotel—"Carmen's Inn"—Shadowy Balconies—Richly Carved Beds—Rickety Furniture—The Ills that the Flesh is Heir to—Electric Lights —Murat Halstead and the Food in Manila.

WHERE is Manila? Very few Americans had given the question sufficient thought to answer when our guns broke the silence of years amidst these far-off islands of the Pacific.

Manila is just six hundred and thirty miles beyond the worst bit of sea the globe possesses—six hundred and thirty miles south-east from Hong Kong. To reach it one must take a small ship, wretchedly uncomfortable, that the waters will pitch and toss about until life seems scarce worth the living even to those who are not seasick. This China Sea is never quiet. From November to March the north-east monsoon blows the ocean into quaking, shivering, tossing mountains; from June to October the south-west monsoon tears these mountains into tatters; and in the interim, in spring and fall, the typhoons prevent any peaceful moment for this wretched sea. I have traversed all the waters of the globe, but must bestow the palm upon this for all that is horrible, not even excepting that bit of ocean the Tasman Sea—which rolls between Australia and New Zealand. In time there will be larger ships placed upon this line, with which, let us trust, other lines will enter into competition, but, up to date, the entire transportation business to the islands has been in the hands of one or two companies that have paid no attention to the passenger department. However, until the famous battle of the 1st of May, passengers for the Philippines were few in number. Spain did not encourage the world at large to enter her Eastern possessions, and if the traveller insisted upon going there his stay was not made pleasant for him.

For two days and three nights we roll and toss about, and then the waters quiet somewhat, until peace, in the shape of the harbour of Manila, relieves us at last. We enter the bay before the dawn has given light enough to show us where we are. As it increases, Dewey's fleet and Cavite are discernible off to the south, while to the westward distant mountains circling north and south enclose a wide and fertile valley where stands the city of Manila. Manila from the sea presents a strong resemblance to Florence, a likeness which is strengthened by its many domes and campaniles, and by its river, but these mountains are more majestic than those around the "fairest city of the earth."

Old Manila occupies a point on the left bank of the river and faces the bay. It is a collection of churches, palaces, and public buildings. Being doubly walled and doubly moated, and surrounded by earthen embankments, it is a place most difficult to capture if properly defended. From the decks of this ship I can see four great Krupp guns, which alone could have done good service, but our Admiral's threat, to "bombard the city if they were used," kept them silent. The modern town stretches away on either side and completely encloses the ancient sections. Viewed from the water, the whole presents an interesting and imposing panorama, from which the glittering banner of the American nation, floating from every available point, in no way detracts.

We are again impressed by the independence of the steamship line when the question of landing comes up.

"Captain, how are we to get ashore?"

"Don't know, my dear sir; the line only contracts to bring you here, not to get you ashore."

"But what are we to do?"

"I really can't say. There may be some sampans along after a while with which you can make a bargain."

No sign of such means of landing is in sight, however, to relieve the minds of the twenty-five passengers. Fortunately, Mr. Wilson of Manila is on board, and when his steam launch comes down, he kindly asks all who desire to go back with him; and so, landing in this new city of ours, we make our way, with the assistance of some dozen or more porters, to the Oriente Hotel. What an establishment! How shiftless and dirty, and how it smells! The building itself is well enough, being large and airy, but it is conducted on the Spanish plan of dirt and sloth, by a manager whose watchword has evidently been *mañana* for all the years of his life. Now, he is forced to deal with a people who insist that all things be done, completed, finished, the day before yesterday. The result to his dead brain is almost insanity. He looks at us in a dazed manner and moans out that he has no rooms, muttering constantly the one all-expressive word, *Americanos, Americanos.* From behind the long line of lattice doors, all up and down the hall, come to our ears words and tones of voices that reduce space to nothingness, and transport us into our own land once more. We secure breakfast, or an apology for one, and in the dining-room entirely forget the fact that there is little to eat, and that little very dirty, as we gaze at our countrymen in wonder and listen to their speech. I have never experienced a more singular sensation than that produced by the sound of our American accent in this far-off corner of the world. These people certainly are of our own land, and any doubt thereof is promptly dispelled by the many questions they ask us about "home." As we answer, I gaze at their fresh, clear, energetic faces, and then at those of the dark-skinned, lazy servants and manager, and wonder how the juxtaposition came about. What decree of fate demanded that our fresh, young nation should come out of the east and destroy forever the last remnants of the once great colonial empire of Charles V.? Yet that decree has gone forth, and here we are in full possession of ancient Manila.

Breakfast—save the name!—being disposed of, we sally forth to look for rooms, but even with that necessary task on hand, I cannot but pause and gaze on the scene before me. This is the principal square of the new city, on one side of which stretches a vast tobacco warehouse, where excellent cigars can be bought for a song—$25 in gold per thousand. To our left rises one of the great churches, and through its portals, in the shadowy interior, gleam the lights of many candles, while the fragrance of incense floats outward toward us over the heads of the bowing worshippers. Beggars crowd the portals, dirt and dust cover the pavements sacred and profane. The centre of the square, meant originally to be ornamental, is wholly neglected, and wretched to look upon. Through the streets rush all sorts and conditions of vehicles. I use the word "rush" advisedly, because no one ever drives slowly in Manila, not even excepting the evening pleasure-seekers in the Luneta; all move at a breakneck pace. Even the tram-cars, drawn by three sturdy little stallions, speed wildly along, so that it would be impossible to board them while in motion.

The streets of Manila are crowded throughout the day until 10 P.M. Travellers generally use a victoria drawn by smart little ponies, the rig costing four dollars in gold per day. The native cart, the *carromato*, is a rough, high-wheeled vehicle on two wheels, with a square body or platform around which runs a railing a foot in height; upon this are placed the seats—merely loose boards. This cart is hauled

A "CARROMATO," MANILA.

by one horse. There is also a neat carry-all with two seats, facing each other, which one enters at the rear, and which somewhat resembles our railway cabs. There is a third kind of carry-all, called *quilez,* which has but one seat close behind the small perch for the driver. Amidst all the bustle of the streets I notice but one vehicle that does not tear along at a breakneck pace, and that is the cart drawn by native oxen. Fright will sometimes start these animals, however, and when it does, all else goes down before them.

We stop at the English Hotel in the Escolta—Manila's principal street. I secure a front room and spend much time hanging out of the windows, and, for the panorama offered therefrom, I forgive the house many of its shortcomings. It is truly a Spanish inn, just such as Carmen was wont to meet her lover in. We almost expect to be hailed by her from out the shadowy balconies surrounding its courtyard, which should echo to the sound of the guitar and the patter of dancing feet rather than to the clank of American sabres; but at least the sabres mean protection and not robbery and assassination, and the "Carmens" are not all in Spain. From the centre of the court rise some battered old trees with wide tables built around their roots, while opening off the wide galleries one finds the dining and bedrooms. There are not more than a dozen in all of the latter very unique apartments. There is never any lock to their doors, mine being provided, because I insist upon it, with a peg, whereby I can bar entrance by night. The floors are bare and very dirty. Clean towels, etc., are unknown, and no chair possesses more than three legs. But one gazes in amazement at the beds. Stately, carved structures with canopies, some of them would be ornamental in any house. They have cane bottoms, across which are stretched fine mats of Manila straw; these are covered with sheets, which, with pillows, form the entire equipment. One never needs any covering, save perhaps a corner of the sheet.

If you ask for tea in the morning, the article brought you reduces you to such a state of hopeless despair that words fail to relieve your feelings, and, no matter how full your vocabulary might be, the boy would not understand you. He may bring you a spoon, but that is rarely done. However, if the stuff is hot, drink it and be thankful.

The flesh is heir to many ills in the tropics, and some of the lesser ones attack the stranger at once and are the hardest to endure. The very clothes fresh from the laundry are in league against his peace and quiet. These people never use hot water in their laundry-work, but generally go to a dirty stream where a parasite of some sort is soaked into the garments with the result, to the wearer, that wherever they chafe the person through perspiration or friction a scarlet rash will appear which burns intolerably, is most unpleasant, and, unless attended to, will extend over the entire body. Chemists tell me that strangers are more liable to its attack than natives. I should fancy that our army must suffer greatly from this. It undoubtedly comes from using foul water, as a sunny, hot day will cause your clothing to become so offensive

THE ESCOLTA, MANILA.

that it must be removed. But to return to the house.

As night comes on, I look around for the tallow dip, by which I had fancied light would be furnished, when I am astonished by a sudden blaze of electricity, and discover that the whole of the wretched hostelry, as well as the entire city, is lighted by the genius of Edison.

As for the meals!—I do not blame my good friend and neighbour, Murat Halstead, sick as he was, from fleeing away in despair. The food is horrible, but let it pass. Fortunately for me I have little to do with it, as, having been "put up" at the English Club at Malate and the Tiffin Club in the city, and having friends in the army, I am rarely here except to sleep.

CHAPTER XV

DAILY LIFE IN "BINONDO"

Streets of Manila—English Club—Noises and Diseases—A Drive into the Insurgents' Territory—Aguinaldo's and General Otis's Proclamations—Reports from Iloilo—Refusal of Press there to Print the President's Proclamation—Spanish Officers and Soldiers—The Former together with the Friars to Blame for Much of the Present Trouble—An Invitation to a Ball on the "to-be-Captured" *Olympia*—Rumours of an Attack—Closing of the Shops in the City—A General Call to Arms—Wild Scene in the Escolta—The Water-Supply and its Exposed Condition—Sam Paloc and its Desecrated Graves—Attack on one of our Sentries, and Death of the Tagalos—The 14th Regulars—"Retreat"—The "Angelus" and the *Star-Spangled Banner*.

THE streets of Manila are wide for the most part, its houses are nearly all two-storied and square, with the second story extending over the sidewalk. In the resident portions of the town there are handsome villas and fine grounds. The English Club, a pleasant building, and most hospitably open to strangers who are properly introduced, is beautifully placed by the sea in Malate, to the south of the old town. Broad avenues stretch away in all directions, and every now and then the traveller comes across an ancient church with its clanging bells. But Manila cannot compare with the City of Mexico, though it claims almost as many inhabitants—three hundred and fifty thousand.

Save during the heat of the day, the streets are crowded with vast concourses of people. The several lines of street-cars are always jammed and are already covered with American advertisements. Hackney carriages, capable of carrying two people, have six or eight natives crowded into them. Owing to the prevalence of small-pox, one avoids these vehicles and also the street-cars. At certain times of the day there are not enough of both to carry the moving population. In our drive of yesterday we crossed into the insurgents' territory and drove where we pleased without heed or hindrance; on the contrary, we were saluted wherever we went, notwithstanding the fact that Aguinaldo had issued the previous day his proclamation of "Liberty or Death."

The proclamation of General Otis with that of the President was issued first, and it seems to be the opinion of the English and Americans here that the Tagalos do not understand it. Some claim that it is in fact just what they want, while others hold that nothing short of anarchy and confusion will satisfy the so-called leaders; but all agree that they are fools indeed not to accept our terms. Many fear that Aguinaldo's proclamation means the beginning of a long guerrilla war, carried on through mountains and swamps where our men cannot exist, but where the insurgents can fight from behind barriers of some sort, and never in the open; a war in which we may need at least fifty thousand troops, as many black ones as possible, for they can better endure the summer heat of these islands.

To-day's report from Iloilo is to the effect that no press would print General Otis's proclamation, and it was perforce done by typewriters and read aloud, only to be ridiculed by the people, who in reply told our men to issue all the proclamations they desired, and do what they desired, but not to land one soldier or there would be bloodletting.

Bound by instructions from Washington to have no "bloodshedding" unless actually attacked, our forces were tied hand and foot, and the people, knowing nothing of the cause, set down our inaction to cowardice. At least this proclamation of Aguinaldo's was attributed directly to our supposed supineness, or, as they called it, "cowardice," at Iloilo.

As we drive along we pass numbers of insurgents all over the city. They are allowed the freedom of the town until sunset, so long as they go unarmed. The Spanish officers are all out on parole, but their soldiers are restricted to the old city, and both "must be in quarters at eight o'clock." They are quartered to the number of eight thousand all over the old town, while the cathedral is but a barracks, which seems a shame.

It is the general opinion that we owe much of the present condition of affairs with the revolutionists to the Spanish officers and priests. The former, being on parole, spread poison on all sides—ditto the priests. After all, we must remember that the ties between the natives and the Spaniards are very strong—they have the same religion, and there is much mingling of blood and language. We are outsiders, and, like the Irishman's wife, they will turn against us. They have no love for nor belief in us, and cannot appreciate what we would do for them.

Just before the battle of May 1st, the Spanish Admiral appeared one evening on the Escolta. He was in all the glory of full dress, and proceeded to harangue the multitudes, assuring them that his fleet would promptly sink the "tin kettles" of the Yankees, while he had numberless prisons prepared in the old fortress for the "American pigs." It is also said that invitations had been issued to the "first Spanish families," inviting them to a ball on the "to-be-captured *Olympia*." The Escolta rang with cheers for old Spain and the brave Admiral.

Rumours of trouble are rife to-day in the Escolta; many actually believe that the insurgents mean to attack the city at once, and most of the shops are closed for fear of looting. It has been a strange awakening for this sleepy old town, and some of her people have risen to the occasion and are making money. Every other shop in this street has been turned into a beer hall, and all are full of a motley crowd. Through the door of yonder spacious place, the "Alhambra," I can see Spaniards, Tagalos, Chinese, French, and Americans, and our uniforms are to be seen everywhere.

Some few days after the fall of the city, a Spanish paper printed a view of the appearance of the Escolta under Yankee rule. All down each side of its narrow, crooked way could be seen over almost every door "Bar," "Bar," "Bar." It is not much better now, but the regulations are better, and these places are closed at 10 P.M. and on Sundays.

There are some hundreds of our men in yonder Alhambra, and even as I write come the notes of a general alarm. At its summons a rush for the street ensues, which completely wrecks the establishment, while the passage of our men up the Escolta causes the natives the greatest terror, and their puny figures flee in all directions before the onward rush of our giants. The city has become a scene of the wildest confusion, and much of it, as I watch from my window on the Escolta, is very amusing.

The entire life of the streets rushes in one direction, while that of the pavements takes the other, especially the Spanish officers, who make a desperate attempt to get into the old walled town, well knowing what their fate will be if the Tagalos obtain the upper hand. They are, however, all stopped by the sentries at the Spanish Bridge, and I can plainly see their wild gesticulations and arguments, all of which produces no effect on the crossed bayonets of our men. In the midst of the confusion a lot of Chinese, with their dancing-master steps and bland smiles, come sailing around a corner, each bearing burdens at either end of long poles over their shoulders. They go down bag and baggage like a pack of cards, and are blown away like the leaves of autumn, vainly endeavouring to grab at their sticks, rags, and tatters, while their chatter changes to the clatter of a flock of frightened geese. The shops of the Escolta close as by magic, their owners repairing to the second-story windows. It takes but about fifteen minutes for our entire twenty thousand men to get to position, so perfectly has the city been mapped out and each squad and sentinel assigned to position.

For half an hour the town appears devoid of all life, and then, the alarm passing, the tide of humanity flows on once more. The shops open, the concert halls tune up, and all is merry.

The cause of the disturbance to-day, and the consequent general call to arms, will probably remain a mystery—at least there are so many reasons given that the truth is hopelessly lost. Some attribute it to the raiding of a gambling hell in the old town, during which the only victim was a dog. Horse thieves are talked of and many other causes, but, whatever the true cause, General Otis considered it sufficiently important to send in a general call. But my carriage is ready for another drive.

Almost the first thing a traveller notices is the unprotected state of the water-works and -mains. Manila's water-supply is brought to the city from a distance of seven miles, through large iron pipes on the surface of the ground. Its source and the pipes for the greater part of the way are within the insurgents' territory, and it is a marvel that they have never interfered with the system during all these years of trouble with Spain. But they never have done so, the reason given being their desire to spare their families and friends living in the city.

I am told that I cannot travel in the country, that Aguinaldo will not permit it, yet we drive daily far beyond our outposts, and we pass hundreds of insurgents, who simply salute. On the drive to-day we visit the Chinese cemetery, some miles beyond our sentries. The spot is as desolate as such spots

9

usually are, but it is on the only rising ground around Manila, affording an extensive prospect east, north, and south over rich plains and lovely mountains, and westward over the city and bay. Around our feet are scattered the white tombs of the dead, the Tagalos burying in catacombs and graves, while the Chinese, even those who are Christians, still cling to the queer, round-topped tombs so dear to the Celestials, and upon which the emblem of Christianity seems strangely out of place.

The scenes in these *campos santos* are often terrible to look upon. Here before us is a catacomb of a native, ruthlessly broken open by some vandal, with its coffin torn asunder, displaying the features of an old man. The wind lifts his snowy locks as I glance inward, and seems to moan in protest at the desecration of his last sleep, at this horrible barbarity. The old man has been buried with care; he was somebody's loved one, so I try to give him the shelter of his coffin lid, but it is useless, and the custodian laughs at me for my pains. Coming from a country where the dead are treated with all reverence, the callous indifference of these people to those they have lost strikes one as horrible; but how much more horrible the actions of their priesthood, who, unless the five dollars yearly are paid for a grave, will ruthlessly tear it open and cast the remains into the horrible Golgotha!

We visit also the Campo Santo of Sam Paloc, the burial-place of the native poor; a vast, neglected square where both Spaniards and insurgents have camped time and again. The chapel is wrecked, and hundreds of graves and catacombs have been

SANTALON ROAD, WITH WATER WORKS MAIN, MANILA.

rifled and desecrated. One corner of the wall is broken down and transformed into an earthwork, just outside of which stand some of our pickets, and, as we chat with them, our eyes rove afar inland, over a lovely landscape of green fields and waving trees stretching away to where the foot-hills rise to a union with the higher mountains, spreading off range after range—a peaceful scene save where our soldiers show forth, and where the insurgent lines stand out in the underbrush. Last night two of the insurgents approached an American soldier, and after the salutation of *Filipinos amigos*, stabbed him in the cheek. He promptly shot them dead, and they now lie in yonder hut awaiting burial.

During our return drive we pass several barracks full of insurgents and within easy range of their forts, but no motion, friendly or hostile, is made. A wide sweep east and south of the city brings us to the barracks of the 14th in Malate, just in time to hear "retreat" sounded for the night. The evening drill takes place in front of a statue of Queen Isabella, which stands near an old church. It is a strange sight to watch the long lines of American soldiers, to hear our language on all sides, and then to look around at the crowds of dark-skinned natives, at the lounging Spanish officers and insurgents, and, finally, at the placid face of the Queen where she gazes outward over the bay, in grave amazement, as it were, at the presence of Dewey's fleet down near Cavite. Soon the clattering, cracked bells of the ancient church ring out the "Angelus," and as it ends the notes of the *Star-Spangled Banner* float out on the evening air, while our flag comes slowly down for the night. Westward the waters of the bay glisten and quiver in the sunset. The sky is all aflame, with Dewey's ships silhouetted against the crimson glow, but ships and crimson vanish suddenly as the curtain of night falls on Malate.

CHAPTER XVI

OLD MANILA

Old Manila—Effect of the Earthquakes—Gloom of the Ancient City—Ruins of Churches and Convents—The Official Palace—Statue of Magellan—Portraits of Old Spaniards—Portrait of the Queen and King—View from the Palace Windows—The Cathedral—Desecration of the Edifice by the Prisoners—Monkeys on the High Altar—Jewels on the Shrines.

MANILA is called the Venice of the far East, probably because there is no resemblance to the "Bride of the Adriatic." The old city alone is known as "Manila." All the other sections are called by separate names. The walls of the ancient town were built in 1590. Standing on the left bank of the river, and close to the bay, they are the first object to attract the traveller's notice. There are eight drawbridge entrances through them, and, until 1852, the draws were raised and gates were closed from 11 P.M. until 4 A.M.; but an earthquake in that year destroyed a portion of one of the gates, and thereafter the town was decreed open all the time.

In the great earthquake of 1863 the shock lasted half a minute, causing four hundred deaths, while two thousand were wounded by falling buildings.

The loss was estimated at $8,000,000. Forty-six public and five hundred and seventy private buildings were totally wrecked. This earthquake caused the abandonment of tiles as roofing, galvanised iron being substituted.

The shock of 1647 destroyed all the churches but two, and all the monasteries but one. The shock of 1863 brought down all the churches again, so that there are no old edifices. The façades of some, however, survived both shocks. The ancient city is sombre and gloomy, and is without popular cafés, opera-house, theatre, or place of amusement. All the trading, all the banks, all the business houses, theatres, and hotels—all the life, in fact—are in the section on the island of Binondo, just opposite the old town and on the right bank of the river.

Old Manila is laid off in squares, the streets being comparatively wide, and the paving not bad. There are narrow sidewalks, shaded by the projecting roofs of the houses and palaces which rise in regular rows on either side, but never to more than two stories in height; the stories are, however, very high, so that the buildings are not squat, but handsome and stately in appearance, especially the property of the priests. Here and there the traveller will come across evidences of the great earthquake of 1863. Yonder is an entire square shaken into chaos. A stately church with its attendant cloisters and monasteries once stood there, but nothing save the strong outer walls and some of the arches have withstood the shaking of the earth, and the whole is now a picturesque ruin, covered with clambering vines.

Near by I come upon another enclosure, surrounded by a very high wall, with but one entrance. One of our sentries stands on guard, and I ask him what it is.

"Don't know, sir, though I have often wondered at the queer old place."

On entering, I discover that it must have been a group of buildings similar to the first, but now it is one vast tenement-house for the very poor, who cluster around its arches and ruined corridors by the hundreds. One is not tempted to penetrate into its vileness farther than the outer quarter.

The antiquary will find few quainter places on the globe than the old city of Manila, and to him it will be a pleasure to wander up and down her long, gloomy streets, peering into each court and patio, or gazing upward at some richly carved, ecclesiastical façade, perhaps all that the trembling earth spared of a sacred edifice, save some lonely pillars covered with trailing vines. The wine-shops are many, and the guitar tinkles throughout the length and breadth of the town, except where the high walls of the monasteries and convents stare blankly forth.

The streets of old Manila are all at right angles. If I remember correctly, this is the case with all Spanish cities. I can recall none that have crooked streets, unless it be Havana.. Old Manila presents an attractive but not a majestic panorama. There are no soaring spires, or domes, or campaniles, but above its wide moats and massive double walls rise the roofs of its churches, palaces, monasteries, and convents, long, low, and gloomy-looking, save where the brilliant colouring of the walls beneath catches the sunlight. The palaces and private edifices rise just high enough to allow one balcony to overlook the battlements, and, except where the walls of the fortress rise, dark and sombre, these balconies are everywhere, that is, on the outer sides toward the sea and the new city; and as the sun declines they become peopled with pretty maidens, ugly old women, sleek, unctuous-looking friars, Spanish prisoners, and American soldiers, while above all floats that "flag like a flower" brought by a nation out of the east.

General Otis and dozens of our officers have their official quarters in the palace of old Manila—the private palace of the Spanish Governor is located in the outer town; the old building faces what was intended as the main square of the city, with the cathedral filling part of another side. The palace is a large two-storied structure, with all the offices and state apartments on the second floor. This is the case with all buildings, public and private.

We enter a spacious vestibule and ascend a wide staircase which branches at a landing for the second floor. Here we pause a moment to inspect an imposing marble statue of Magellan before passing through a lofty portal into what must have been the hall of audience. The hall itself, a majestic apartment over one hundred feet long by fifty wide, has a beautiful parquet floor, and its lofty walls are lined with long rows of life-size portraits of Spain's famous men; here again we see the features of Magellan—a typical Spanish face and one interesting to look upon. His eyes seem to follow us with interest as we pass down the long apartment; evidently he does

GRAND STAIRCASE, OFFICIAL PALACE, MANILA.

not recognise our faces as belonging to his native land, or to that for which he toiled, suffered, and died, but his glance is not unfriendly; certainly his expression is in no degree as sinister or suspicious as those of the long line of notables which keep him company.

This is the heart of old Manila. In this room all the gay festivities must have taken place, all the intrigues, all the plots and counter-plots of those who have held the destinies of these islands in their hands for three hundred years. I cannot learn the age of this building, but the spot is and always has been the site of the official palace.

Passing out of the grand hall and upward to the main floor, the traveller enters the council chamber, and is confronted by a chair of state over which hangs a portrait of the good Queen Regent and the little King, and I think it is safe to say that each and every American takes off his hat to Christina, and has a smile for the little King. The room is furnished by a large and elaborately carved table and some dozen or so of heavily carved chairs of teak-wood, each bearing the royal arms. This, with the gallery, forms the main apartment of the palace, but there are many others opening off of the long halls surrounding the inner court.

The council chamber overlooks the square, now a desolate plaza with a few melancholy trees occupying its centre, while in one corner is a crazy campanile, or rather a scaffold, which holds the bells of the cathedral. The original campanile, shattered by earthquakes, stands near by.

The cathedral itself rises on the west, and beyond

are what must be the ruins of the older structure, also shaken down in the disturbance of 1863. Off to the right in the arsenal, where a dress parade of some of our regulars is taking place, one hears the notes of *Marching through Georgia* mingling with the clangour of the bells from the Convent of Santa Clara, whose long roofs rise behind massive walls on the extreme right.

But let us enter the cathedral. It is a building of stately proportions, being some three hundred feet long by one hundred and fifty wide, with a nave, choir, and two transepts, also two side aisles, and a dome of some majesty. There are many frescoes and altars, and, as in all Spanish churches, the centre is closed off into a smaller place of worship, which of course mars the effect, as from no point can be obtained a general view of the whole edifice. But as I walk through it to-day I am desirous only of getting out again. Numberless Spanish soldiers are here, there, and everywhere, lying asleep on the high altar and side shrines, using the sacred edifice in every possible and filthy manner, while pests of monkeys climb over everything; yonder is one lying asleep on the spot where, of old, the host stood in its jewelled monstrance. The floor is slimy with accumulated filth, and the whole is desecrated. I am told that this occurred before our occupation, that the Church abandoned the edifice upon some difficulty with the people, and that Spain first used it as a prison for the insurgents. Certainly the Anglo-Saxon race has never been given to the desecration of churches, save in the time of religious wars, and our authorities would be the last to

CATHEDRAL OF MANILA—EARTHQUAKE RUINS IN FOREGROUND.

countenance such conditions as exist in the old cathedral of Manila to-day. It should not be allowed to continue; there are other places for these prisoners—the buildings of the Convent of Santa Clara, for instance.

St. Andrew is the patron saint of Manila, and his day was duly celebrated by High Mass in this cathedral. He is supposed to have saved the city from the Chinese, and therefore, in bygone years, the priesthood have asserted the supremacy of the Church over the State by spreading the nation's banner over the floor of this edifice for the archbishop to walk over. This custom has since been changed to a procession in which the banner is carried in front and is three times dipped to the image of Christ.

Vast sums of money have been expended in the adornment of the sacred images of the church. Foreman tells us that on All Saints' Day such crowds of people attend the shrines to pray for the dead that Chinese coolies are employed to clear them out every few moments.

CHAPTER XVII

RAMBLES IN OLD MANILA

Attack of the Chinese in 1574—Ambition of the Clergy—Dishonesty of Churchmen and Statesmen—Trials of the Governors for Stealing—Governor-General and his Reputation—His Wife and the Jewels—The Apportionment of the Land by the Patriot Leaders to Themselves—Ignorance of the People on the Subject—The Jesuits and their Monastery—Age of Manila's Churches—The Fortress of Old Manila—The "Black Hole" and its Victims—Armament of the Fort—Officers' Club in the Fortress—Pretty Maidens—Ugly and Slovenly Older Women—The Paseo and Luneta—Gorgeous Sunsets- Wonderful Display of the Fireflies.

THE famous attack of the Chinese occurred in 1574, and the Spaniards were as unprepared then as they were in these latter days. The enemy penetrated within the very walls of the city before the Governor-General would believe that an attack was intended. Then the people fled to Fort Santiago. Cavite saw at that time also a waiting fleet, but though fleet and army both attacked the city, the Spaniards finally gained the victory; the Chinese leader, however, actually obtained admittance to the fortress.

That curse of the Spanish nation—internal dissension—gave little peace to Manila in the years that followed, and even then the immoderate ambition of the clergy had commenced that work which in the end wrecked the happiness of the archipelago. Peculations, frauds, jealousies, and quarrels among both secular and religious bodies had commenced even in 1598. A governor-general was not allowed to depart without an inquiry, generally very necessary, to twist his official neck, and few escaped their enemies at such a time, were they guilty or innocent. The records of Manila show the trials of governor after governor for fraud and stealing. Torralba, in 1717, was charged with stealing $7,000,000. Condemned to pay a heavy fine and to banishment from the Philippines and Madrid, he died in poverty in the hospital; but both before and after him the records are no better, down to our own day. The power of these governors was absolute, and they were often the executioners of the guilty—as in the case of De Lua in 1622, who, suspecting his wife of infidelity, called his priest to confess both the woman and her paramour, after which he (the husband) stabbed them both. The house of the lover was razed to the ground and salt was strewn over the site. The husband continued to govern for two years and then died of melancholy.

In our day one of the governors has left a lasting fame behind him. It is stated here that he appropriated some four million Mexican dollars for his use, and that was but one of his many venal acts. His wife worked hand and glove with him, and the two got all they could. For instance, it was customary to present to the wife of the new governor-general a necklace of jewels, and three were sent to this woman for her selection. She kept them all. If she saw any ornament upon a native, half-caste, or Spaniard which she admired, she would ask to look at it and would then remark, "I like this. I shall keep it." She sold the positions within the grip of her husband to the highest bidder. Small wonder that the honest members of the Spanish Cortes, in open session, called this man a "thief and liar."

That which the rulers of these islands have practised for three centuries has been well learned by the natives; they know no other method, and, to-day, the so-called "patriot leaders" have mapped off most of the rich haciendas, allotting an equal number to each of their members; if successful in driving out our forces they will then be able to sell out at a higher figure. Of course, if we hold the islands this will not work—hence their determination to be independent. If all this could be explained to the people the cause of the "patriots" would collapse, but it cannot. No native paper will publish it, and the people could not read it if this were done.

I sat for an hour to-day in the parlour of the Jesuit monastery talking to the Father Superior and several of the brethren. One of the latter spoke some English, but a continuous residence of twenty-five years had banished most of it from his memory. The room we were in was the only spot in the building not profaned by the war. All the corridors and apartments were full of Spanish prisoners, and paintings of long-dead saints, popes, and padres gazed down in wonder at the sights and sounds which had invaded their solitude.

SAN JUAN DEL MONTE, THE OLDEST CHURCH IN MANILA.

Outside in the courtyards and cloisters resounded the noise of hundreds of voices, but the peace and quiet of the past lingered in this parlour and in the great church adjoining. It is here that I learn from the Father Superior that all the churches of Manila were shattered and thrown down by the trembling earth in 1863. This and all the others, including the cathedral, date from 1867. Naturally this detracts from our interest and we take our departure, making our salutations to the white-robed fathers, who stand with clasped hands at the head of the grand staircase, looking strangely out of place surrounded by all this Babylon of war, and surely holding nothing in common with the condemned friars.

The fortress, we find, with the city walls, is the only portion of the old town which dates from before the earthquake. It is situated at the angle of the river and the bay, and in its walls, which are of enormous thickness, doubtless many relics of Spanish barbarity would come to light if a systematic examination were attempted. The donjons show traces of having been closed up in many places, and, probably, as at the Convent of Santo Domingo in Mexico, many a ghastly horror would be exposed by opening these places. There are several visible donjons, dark and dank enough for all purposes, and in one of them, called the "Black Hole," more than one hundred political prisoners were shut down, most of whom perished. Another, fifteen by forty feet, held eighty poor wretches upon whom the door had been closed and they had been "forgotten." All were suffocated. Better, surely, the fate of those who were shot to death out on the fashionable drive, a sight that people were wont to drive to as they now do to listen to the music.

This old fort is doubly moated and thickly walled. It is an enlarged St. Augustine. There are some good guns upon the walls, but they show no evidence of having been used or that any attempt was made to do so. In the court of the arsenal, outside the main portal,—an archway richly decorated with the arms of Spain,—are quantities of fine shot and shell piled in symmetrical rows and pyramids, and all undisturbed; indeed, it is said that this ammunition will not fit any of the guns in the city. Inside of one courtyard stands a poor Filipino who murdered a man not long since. He has been tried and the evidence sent to Washington, but let us hope that his case will not be passed upon as though he were a white man; he knew not what he did. As I passed him he fairly grovelled on the ground. He sleeps at night, and has done so for a month, in one of the old donjons of the fortress.

The officers at the citadel have very pleasant quarters. They have formed a club, the main room of which, located on the city walls, overlooks all the river with its shipping, and the modern city with its life bubbling over the Spanish Bridge.

There are certain inhabitants of the citadel which apparently object most strongly to our occupation, as upon the slightest relaxation of vigilance they descend in numbers and steal everything in sight—small monkeys, which run shrieking and chattering all over the fortress. All sorts of traps have been laid for them, and great has been the harvest. I counted ten shut up in one small closet, all of which had been captured on the previous day. Many of them have been domesticated, but with sad results, as no amount of Western education will make a monkey honest. The little creatures chatter and threaten us as we pass out into the streets of the city. The sun is towards his setting, and we leave the shadows of the old town to enjoy the spectacular display he is sure to offer ere he goes to rest. The city has awakened and is preparing to follow us.

As the cool hours of the day approach, one will note in the old town the appearance at the windows of many a sweet-faced, dark-eyed Spanish beauty, and often, in the shadows of the street, can be seen her silent lover, for thus, from afar, is the courting done in Spanish lands. Day after day they will gaze at each other from a distance, and all the while the old duenna sits just behind the girl in the shadow of the casement. If the young people decide—silently, it must be—to carry matters further, the lover approaches the father, but not until the full betrothal is he allowed to converse with his lady-love. These Spanish beauties soon lose all trace of good looks, and I fancy it is largely owing to the life they lead, which consists in doing nothing all day long, sleeping just as long as possible, and only waking up to dress and drive when the sun is setting. As they grow older and are married, they become more and more slovenly. It is a common sight here to see a carriage in the Luneta with three pretty girls, neatly dressed, attended by a mother or older married sister, perfect slovens; looking as though they had not dressed at all, and as if the simple removal of a dirty, loose-fitting wrapper would find them ready for bed. As for fresh water, they certainly know little about it, and if you sail on a Spanish ship you will find the bathrooms used as storerooms, or, if the ship is crowded, with beds made on or in them. But let us pass outward to the "Rotten Row" of Manila.

The Paseo de Santa Lucia and the Luneta, forming together the fashionable drive of Manila, extend from the river along the bay for about two miles. Starting at the monument of Simon de Anda, the former runs for the first mile in front of the old city, the deep moat of which bounds it on the left. There the ancient town is seen to the best advantage, as its forts, palaces, cathedrals, bishop's palace, and the new and very splendid buildings of the St. Augustines front that side. The more the traveller contemplates that old town the greater becomes his amazement that a place so capable of stubborn defence was so promptly surrendered—but it *has* surrendered, its gates all stand wide open, and from them pour a steady stream of vehicles, while its walls are thronged with American and Spanish soldiers, the latter prisoners in name, watching the passing crowd or the panorama of city, river, bay, and distant mountains.

This avenue is bordered with palm trees, but the flowers have been neglected. Indeed, the Botanical Gardens on the other drive have been entirely destroyed, the trees having been cut down to afford a better outlook from the forts. Admiral Dewey's fleet is visible down the harbour, while southward, near the suburbs of Malate, the monitor *Monadnock*

WALLED CITY AND BISHOP'S PALACE FROM THE LUNETA, MANILA.

has drawn near the coast and trained her guns on the approach to the city. They say that the first appearance of those engines of destruction, the monitors, sailing past fort and city ended all thoughts of resistance, yet there are four great Krupp cannon yonder that with the proper men behind them could greatly have troubled the *Monadnock*, and if Manila had been in the hands of any nation save Spain they would have been used, despite the threats of our Admiral.

On the farther section of this Luneta the military executions used to take place, and, while the band played, the people lined up in their carriages to watch them. Political criminals were generally shot.

As we leave the Luneta and turn towards the city nature puts her most gorgeous colours into the sunset. From the Spanish Bridge the river and shipping are all aflame, while the old walled town rises dark and gloomy above it, until the sun turns the towers and domes into a golden glow. Above, the whole background of the sky is of that fair turquoise blue so beautiful in the dome of heaven, and across its very centre pulsates a wonderful river of rose colour, while trailing banners of the deepest crimson are flaunted far out over a sea dark and mysterious, save where its bosom ever and anon reflects the glory above it.

In the avenues of Malate last evening I witnessed one of the loveliest sights I have ever seen in the tropics. The sunset had faded and night's curtain had descended, when I became aware that an illumination of some extraordinary sort was going on all around me. All the trees great and small up and down both sides of the avenue, and off into the plantations on either hand, suddenly glowed with what seemed to be myriads of small electric lights; little globes as large as a pea hung trembling in countless numbers amidst the dark green leaves, glowing and quivering, and throwing out so much light that the effect was like soft moonlight; it came not from the genius of Edison, however, but from the wondrous storehouse of nature, for those lights were all living fireflies; but the deception was all the greater because, unlike those of other lands, they clung steadfastly to one spot and glowed with a steady silvery light. Nothing in nature could be more beautiful, especially appearing, as it did, out of that deep gloom which in the tropics always follows the gorgeousness of departing day; when, especially here in Manila, the heavens, night after night, declare the glory of God as they rarely seem to do elsewhere on earth. I watched the wonderful spectacle of the fireflies for hours, half expecting to hear fairy music in the enchanted silence, and to see Titania suddenly appear with her winged court.

CHAPTER XVIII

THE FRIARS

The Garrote—The Observatory—The Spanish Bridge—Passage of the Archbishops and Governors-General—The Circuit of the Old City—The Archiepiscopal Residence—That of the Augustines—The Number of these Institutions—Friars of the Fifteenth Century Have Nothing in Common with Enlightened Catholics—The Procurators in Madrid—The Fate of an Enlightened Brother—Power of the Friars over the People—Dishonour—Prison Record of Dorothea Arteaga—Attempt to Serve a Warrant on a Friar—Vowed to Celibacy, but Chastity is Unknown—Boasts of a Friar—Refusal to Bury the Dead—Destruction of the Churches by Infuriated Natives—Names of the Orders—Their Enormous Wealth—The Convent of Santa Clara—A Decoy House—Events of 1888—The Secret Passage—Condition To-day—Attempted Entrance—Chaplain Stevens of the 14th Regulars and his Conflict over the Schoolhouse—Aguinaldo's Refusal and the Archbishop's Commands—Opposition of the Friars to Enlightenment—Reports from Porto Rico—Obligations of our Government—Confiscation of Paco Cemetery—The Golgotha—Purchase of a Cemetery for the Poor—Graves of our Dead in Paco Campo Santo—A Soldier's Funeral.

TO-DAY I visited the prison for the purpose of seeing the garrote, and on asking for it was referred to the office, where for a moment I waited, resting against a wooden upright near the door.

"I would like to see the garrote."

"You are leaning against it, sir."

"That harmless-looking thing?"

"Yes; it has sent over forty into the other world to my knowledge."

It is certainly simplicity itself—a short, square column of wood some four feet high, with a wooden seat on one side. Near the top at the height of a man's neck the column passes through a parallelogram of brass some four inches in width by a foot and a half long, the front of which opens to admit the neck. Through the back of this and through the column of wood passes an iron screw which enters a cross-bar of brass. This slides forward in grooves cut in the inner face of the parallelogram. This cross-bar is round, as is the inner face of the front bar, so that towards the neck, front and back, are presented these two round bars of brass. The back one is shoved forward by a turn of the handle on the other end of the screw, and a half-turn of that handle is sufficient to break the neck and cause instant death. A full turn has been known to sever the head from the body. There is no piercing the neck by a needle or rod, simply this sudden pressure; the head falls forward, the victim gives a gasp, and all is over. Executions by the garrote are said to produce painless, instantaneous death. This instrument looked new and fresh. There were no stains of any sort on its shining metal or wood.

It was pleasant to pass from the contemplation of man's suffering to the calm, pure atmosphere of the observatory, where I was received by two Irish priests who spoke excellent English—perfect, in fact. One of them showed me with justifiable pride the interesting institution which is conducted by the

THE GARROTE, MANILA.

Jesuits. It is young, but seems very full of the finest instruments. Of special interest were those which warn of the coming of typhoons and mark their course, some travelling in vast circles until lost in the Pacific, others moving, apparently, as straight as a crow flies, while others zigzagged in their passage. Earthquakes were also recorded by fine black lines on white paper. The sounds from the underworld are listened for and recorded. You may hear them yourself by the use of those ear-trumpets, but no sound, save when the volcanic forces are at work, ever comes up from the world beneath us. To describe all here would be impossible. The library is very extensive and in good order. Its books are in all languages. Outside, the tower for a large telescope is about completed, the instrument being already in place. The institution is also a school, and has several hundred students. Apparently the priests are in favour of our rule. They spoke as though they were of us, and strongly insisted upon the "establishment of schools as soon as might be for the teaching of OUR language." Their clear faces and bright calm eyes are pleasant to look upon, reminding the traveller of their honourable brethren at home.

The Spanish Bridge connecting the old town with the new is crowded with the passing multitude, who are kept in order by our sentries. The approach on the north is steep, and the little street-cars are drawn up at the usual wild rate of speed, to the incessant tooting of a shrill tin whistle. Manila crowds are democratic in these degenerate days, but had you chanced to pass this way some years since, when Spain and the Church were in full power, you might have witnessed the passing of the Archbishop with his many outriders, and if so, you would have stood still with hat off, or his guards would have knocked it off for you, with no care as to whether or not they knocked your head off. The same ceremony was insisted upon when the Governor-General passed by in his coach.

To-day I saw His Grace the Prelate as he left his palace in the old town—left it quietly and with no state. I had but a glimpse of a large, black-browed and olive-skinned man with a very gloomy expression. To his credit it is stated that, realising the hopelessness of resistance, he urged the surrender of the city in the name of humanity. If the present state of affairs does not please him he has to thank his friars here for it. Had he and his predecessors forced these men to imitate their brethren in England and America, these islands would not have been in the state they are to-day. Leaving the door of his palace, we made the circuit of the old city, passing just inside the walls. The ecclesiastical buildings are many and some are very fine, especially that of the Augustines—which is next to the archiepiscopal residence. The present structure, which has never been finished, and which probably occupies the site of an older one, is used by us for our Spanish prisoners. Its lower story is of dark red marble, while its upper floor, projecting over the pavement, is of wood, richly carved and gilded. A small gallery spanning a narrow street connects this building with the college, whose massive walls, gloomy and forbidding, built like a fortress with iron-barred win-

HEADQUARTERS OF THE AUGUSTINES, MANILA.

dows, have more the appearance of a prison than a college. The entire group reminds the observer of the palace of the Doges, the prison, and the connecting "Bridge of Sighs."

The outer circuit of the city—within the walls—seems given over to these institutions, and as we pass, numbers of friars are visible, showing that many are still left in Manila, though many more have fled. The friars of the Philippines have at all times been the real power in these islands. They do not belong to the present age, but are of the fifteenth century and have nothing in common with the enlightened Catholic Church of Europe and America. They hold allegiance in name only to the Pontiff. They have enormous wealth, and have used it to bribe the authorities at Madrid, who have allowed them to do as they desired. Each order possesses a procurator in the capital, who constantly guards their interests. They have been condemned at all times openly and strongly by respectable members of the Church who have ventured into these islands. If an enlightened, progressive brother was sent out to them he was either returned at once or "disappeared." I am told that this happened but a few years ago.

The story of the deaths of General Solano in 1860 and the Bishop of Cebu in 1873, which occurred so opportunely for the welfare of these monastics, would prove interesting reading. Such has been the power of these friars over these people for centuries, that they—the people—have been led to accept dishonour from them as right and fitting, but they have not always submitted.

There is to be seen among the prison records now in the hands of our authorities, one, a charge of sacrilege against a woman, Dorothea Arteaga, who was charged with stealing a chalice from the altar; but in the account of the trial the real reason—her opposition to dishonour—was given. We are told of another priest, against whom a warrant had been secured by the friends of his victim, who promptly shot the man who attempted to serve it, and threatened to shoot anyone who should repeat the attempt, and that ended the matter.

"Taken as a whole, it would be impossible to speak with too great severity of the disrepute into which the actions of these dissolute men has brought the Roman Catholic religion *in these islands.* A man of God on whom rests the most solemn vows of holiness, chastity, and poverty, living amongst a simple and impressionable race, a monster of iniquity, an extensive landowner nursing his ill-gotten wealth, a monument of lechery and debauch. Let us hasten to add that the Philippine himself is far from being morally immaculate. The priest may take his daughter or his sister and welcome, for the offspring will be a person of such added importance as European blood never fails to give in Eastern countries. But the islander draws the line firmly at his wife and equally firmly at his prospective bride, and it is from wanton straying into these forbidden pastures that the good shepherd has been mainly instrumental in bringing his country into trouble.

"So aggressive indeed have the priests become that cases were actually known where the priest had refused at the altar to marry a couple, having himself there in that holy place cast lecherous eyes over the would-be bride and determined to reserve her for his own base desires. Stories about the priests are so numerous and so well authenticated that it is impossible for any impartial person not to acknowledge that the islanders had just and substantial grounds for including a sweeping indictment of the whole class amongst the main grievances which they had against the Spanish suzerainty." (*The Philippines*, by Major Younghusband, page 14.)

These friars are vowed to celibacy, but make no pretence of leading, or of being expected to lead, chaste or pure lives, and it is a well-known fact that they have kept their mistresses openly, with no attempt at concealment. Foreman in his book—a standard work—on the islands speaks of this, and adds:

" Surely the present state of these islands is due to the pernicious example and influence of these priests. How can anyone expect anything save oppression and robbery when those in charge of their souls' welfare and their hope of a life to come set them so degraded an example! Is it to be wondered at that the Spanish empire fell, and who save the priesthood are to blame therefor?"

An Englishman who has lived in these islands for many years informed me that a friar in his district in the country boasted of his "conquests" among his congregation; the gentleman also stated that his servant one day came to him, complaining that he could not get his child, who had been dead four days, buried, unless he paid the priest $16—out of a salary of $20 per month. His master, becoming indignant, decided to report the case to the Governor, and directed his man to bring the name of the priest; but the latter, getting wind of the matter, buried the child. The dead must be buried in this climate on the day they die, and four days meant a horror for all concerned. These statements, which are but a fraction of the whole, can all be proven, and if those official records are ever printed the civilised world will be horrified. It is certainly better that such things should be made known, better that such actions should be exposed to the condemnation of the whole world, Catholic and Protestant, that not only the transgressors, but also those who have aided and abetted by concealment and otherwise, be impeached.

Many of these friars have now fled from the islands and live in Hong Kong and other cities, but in view of what is known of their horrid lives and terrible practices one forgives the destruction of their churches. The edifices have been desecrated by their presence far more than by the blows of the destroyers, and all the rains of heaven will not wash them pure again. The orders most detested by the people are the Dominicans, Augustines, Franciscans, and Recollets. The Jesuits should not be included, as they are not of that stamp, and a genuine sentiment in their favour exists.

It will be stated in favour of these orders that whatever education or advancement these people possess is due to these instructors; but that all the good they have ever done is wiped out by their acts of robbery, oppression, and degradation is amply proved by the intense hatred of all the people for them—a hatred so bitter that it has extended to the destruction of the churches where their families have worshipped for centuries, to the very dead in their graves.

If the insurgents should drive us out, their first act would be wholesale slaughter of the friars, guilty and innocent, and this we cannot permit. Still, and notwithstanding all this, our Government must remember that these friars will never be friendly to America, because enlightenment and progress mean death and destruction to their power. On the contrary, they will at the first signs of an advance from these insurgents join forces with them at once, trusting to a common religion and language, to like manners and customs, and to old associations to regain for them their lost place and full power.

The wealth of the brethren is enormous here, even though huge sums have been invested elsewhere. They own largely in Hong Kong, Shanghai, and at many other points under the English flag.

I have been told by the general manager in the East of the greatest steamship lines to the East that about the time we captured Manila, the sick in her hospitals were informed by the friars that there was no medicine, nor money with which to buy it, yet at that very time these friars sent $27,000,000 (Mexican) to Shanghai.

They have been an absolute power, bowing to none, as the prison records demonstrate. The memory of the affair of the Convent of Santa Clara, which occurred but ten years since, in 1888, is still fresh in the minds of the English who reside here. It was simply a decoy house into which girls were enticed by the friars, and into which one was decoyed who happened to be more respectable or more independent than the others. The first night she fled shrieking through the building and managed to get out on the roof, where she made herself heard by the patrol, who broke in the door. Manila happened at that time to have an honest, honourable man for governor, who decided to make investigations. A secret passage was found connecting the building with an adjoining monastery. The results of the investigation under the grass of the court-yard scandalised even Manila. The affair was hushed up, however, by the power of the Archbishop.

The Convent of Santa Clara was founded in 1621 by Geronima de la Asuncion, and is to-day still an institution of the Middle Ages. Refusing to admit reforms, she was expelled by the friars, but was afterwards restored for twenty years. Even at that period, public opinion was vividly aroused by the horrible reports about this institution, but how little effect public opinion had is proved by the suppression of the incident of 1888. People in Manila strongly hint that things are not one whit better under its roof to-day than in 1888. It stands within the walls of the old city, close by the official offices of the Governor-General, which are now occupied by General Otis, and consists of a mass of buildings surrounded by a wall thirty feet high, old, dark, and so solid that it has defied the passing of the centuries and the tremblings of the earth which shook the adjacent cathedral into ruins. Over its top rises the dome of the convent church, and the long roofs of the buildings are just visible.

The sun shines down hot and brilliant as we pound on the portal. All Manila has retired for its daily siesta, and our knocking resounds through empty streets and quiet courts with a startling sound. A few dogs rise up to bark at us, but no human being takes note or mark. We are told that the convent at this time is empty, and one of our sentries near by ventures the remark that " none save the dead live there." But there must be a custodian somewhere within, and if so, he shall come forth. Our blows on the ancient portal are renewed again and again, until the solid shutters of a grated casement open about an inch, allowing the sharp nose and black eyes of a gaunt old man to be seen. He regards us in silent wonder for the space of a moment, then, upon seeing that we are bent on an entrance and are of the race of his conquerors, one of us being in uniform, he closes the shutters and opens the door, admitting us to a long, narrow courtyard. On the right rise the high outer walls, on the left the rear of the convent church, and beyond, the buildings of the institution, its long roofs decorated here and there with the emblem of our common religion, strangely out of place in an institution with such a reputation.

We pause to inspect the main portal, a stately structure with pillars and arches. From its niches the statues of many saints gaze down upon us, and all is old, grey, and moss-grown. Like the portals of the churches it is very massive, has evidently stood for many centuries, and is, with some ruined arches, all that has been spared, save the outer walls, by the earthquakes. Passing within, we find ourselves in a lofty, square hall, on whose white walls hangs a large painting of some sacred subject. There is a barred doorway on one side, and a small wicket with a wooden shutter on the other.

Well? We gaze at the old man, and he returns our regard. Then we knock on the door, and his glance changes to one of horror, while the woman who has followed us nearly faints. Suddenly, on the silence which ensues upon our clatter, there arises the sound of women's voices chanting a hymn, and as suddenly the ludicrousness of our position strikes not only ourselves, but the old man and the woman, and in company we sit down and laugh until exhaustion reduces us to silence. The convent is not "empty," and we have with much noise and clamour demanded entrance where no man is supposed ever to have been. The old porter evidently knows the history of the institution, but heretofore the silence of night has shrouded all entrance to this "sacred" institution. Here, however, are two Americans that come at high noon, disturb his slumbers with great clatter, and make no false pretence about their desire and intention of entering this convent of Santa Clara. "What next, what next?"

He continues to chuckle, and the old woman holds up her hands in pretended horror while she casts glances of admiration at my handsome young companion, decked out in a white uniform with gold straps. We wait some time in hopes that the wicket may open and the Lady Abbess look forth, but no sound breaks the intense stillness, even the chanting voices have died away into silence. As we pass out and down the empty courtyard, the custodian takes us into the cool, shadowy church; its high altars are a mass of gilding, flowers, embroideries, and many statues, sacred paintings adorn its walls, and across one end runs the nuns' gallery, enclosed by a fine latticework.

Conveying our thanks in a substantial manner to the old man, we depart, greatly disappointed in not having found the Convent of Santa Clara empty and open for inspection.

So much for the past history of these friars—and, in this connection, it will be well to relate an incident which fully demonstrates the position they have taken towards our people, an incident which came under my personal observation.

Chaplain Pierce of the 14th U. S. Infantry was requested by a delegation of Filipinos to perform certain services, such as the burial of the dead, etc., for them. They were all poor people, and the priests of their Church had refused to bury the dead unless paid for that service, and also to allow a grave unless paid for it. Hence the application to the American chaplain. That the prayer was granted goes without saying. The dead were buried, and that service led to a request by many for religious instruction. A schoolhouse was obtained and a service was held, the service book of the Brotherhood of St. Andrew being used. Promptly the priests began to oppose the measure, and the schoolmaster was ordered to refuse the use of his building. The following Sunday, however, another service was held by the American chaplain, whereupon an application was made to Aguinaldo to forbid it. But, to his credit be it said, he replied that "the patriots had decreed the separation at once and forever of Church and State, and so long as he held command, or could influence matters, this order should be maintained."

The Archbishop was then appealed to, and he ordered the schoolmaster, upon pain of dismissal, to close his house, ordered his simple furniture removed, and the books of the Brotherhood of St. Andrew to be burned. But service was held, no closing or burning was done, and our flag floats over the schoolhouse. It is the old, old story dealt with by all nations, and recently by Mexico—the determination of the ignorant priests to prevent the ingress of all enlightenment, knowing that it means the downfall of their power. In this nineteenth century, in most countries, they have come to the realisation of the fact that the world has advanced beyond the toleration of such actions, and that the intelligent clergy of their Church of to-day will not countenance them. Our Government, if it retains these islands and those of the West Indies, from whence come like reports, must deal with these friars with a strong hand, must force them to leave the islands if they in any way attempt to interfere with the rights of man to worship God as his conscience dictates, or if they do not stop their debauchery of the people. But these friars rest under the impression that the laws of three centuries ago will still be held in force.

The United States Government has confiscated the ancient *campo santo* in Paco—as strange a burial-place as our boys in blue have ever rested in. It stands well without the city, and is unique in form. The *campos santos* of Europe are generally square enclosures, with walls full of catacombs rising tier above tier, the centre being a rank mass of tangled grasses. This one is a vast circle, entered under an ancient, moss-grown gateway, and on either side the walls circle away, pierced like the others by the rows of catacombs; but here there is an inner circle, also entered by an archway, and also full of the catacombs. Facing the entrance and across the centre stands a mortuary chapel where services are held, and behind this are two smaller circles used for the interment of children, while between these is the Golgotha, its stone arch bearing those emblems of mortality, the skull and cross-bones; and on either side of this arch rise two flights of steps. Mounting one of these, the visitor finds himself on the brink of a high semicircular pit, full of the remains of thousands of bodies, all that is left of the poor dead whose relatives have ceased to pay the tax of five dollars per year necessary to their retaining their graves, and so all that is left of them is raked out and cast here, where the sunshine and rain beat them year by year more and more deeply into the dust.

Chaplain Pierce has raised a fund to purchase a spot of ground where the dead may rest until called forth by God, but to do so he was forced to purchase the property through a middleman, a native, the priests having forbidden the sale of all lands to the Americans. Perhaps our Government will stand this, and perhaps it will not. At any rate, it has taken possession of that old *campo santo*, and the mounds that cover our dead boys in blue are rising thick and fast in the centre thereof. From the walls stare the names and titles of Old Spain, names that bring to the mind memories of the gypsies dancing near the Darrow, memories of the Alhambra, of the grim Escorial, or of gay Seville, all dead "for love of country"; but on the marble headstones in the centre one reads names that bring up the wild free life and air of the Rockies, and the life and hope of America. The eyes grow dim as they gaze, blotting out the little flags that already flutter over the grass in this ancient "holy field" of Manila.

As we depart the Dead March sounds upon the air as the funeral cortège of another boy in blue comes slowly in under the old grey archway. We stand with bowed heads as his body is committed to the foreign soil, while that saddest of all melodies, "taps," sounds his requiem. Peace to his ashes and to his soul! Are all the islands of the world worth the destruction of a dozen such as he, or the sorrow that must come down upon his home and kindred, where perhaps his death means the loss of all things?

CHAPTER XIX

THE "BROTHERHOOD OF BLOOD"

Quarters of the 14th Regulars—Dinner at the Mess—Rations of our Army in Manila—The Hospitals and their Corps—Condition of the Men in Manila—Excitement in the City—"Brotherhood of Human Bloodhounds"—The Katipunan Society—Its Origin—Power—Operations against the Spaniards—The First Plot—The Press in Manila—Punishment of a Tagalo by a Soldier.

MUCH of my time is spent with the officers of the 14th Regulars. Their quarters in Malate, close by the waters of the bay, are in a Spanish house, and a private house in Manila is most attractive. There is nothing magnificent about it, but it is very wide, spacious, and airy. In plan it is always square, the second floor, supported by ornamental brackets, overhanging the first some four feet, and, in turn, it is sheltered by a roof with deep eaves. The structure is generally white, or some pale tint, with the panels—it is always built of wood—outlined, and the brackets picked out in bright colours. It is placed well back in the yard, embowered in brilliant flowering shrubs. The second floor is the state floor, and holds all the living-rooms, which are attractive-looking apartments with highly polished parquetry. A wide staircase leads to a large square hall around which the apartments cluster, but so large are the doors of communication that it seems, as regards hall, drawing-room, reception-room, and dining-room, to be one apartment. The bedrooms, of course, are more private, and some are on the ground floor. There is no glass used in the buildings, except in the show-windows of the shops. For a cold night the windows of the dwellings are protected by sliding shutters, the small squares of which are filled with mica or a thin shell. By day the sun is kept out by a set of Venetian slats. When both of these are drawn back the entire house stands open to inspection from the street, and during my constant drives around the city I became intimately acquainted with the domestic arrangements of hundreds of our soldiers. At the headquarters of the 14th Regulars, I can generally tell who is at home without leaving my carriage. The officers are never all there, but someone is sure to be on hand to extend a welcome, which makes Manila seem very near home.

Dinner is generally served at seven o'clock, and the time at the table is spent more in chaff than in disposing of what is set before us. One of the officers, Lieutenant Mitchell, an Irishman, is one of the oldest lieutenants in our army, and has served all through the Civil and Indian wars. He has a full measure of the wit of his native land, and also of its hasty temper, which the other officers delight to ruffle. But all like him. He is a general favourite and will be greatly mourned.* The rations of the mess are all that can be desired—plain, but good,

* Poor fellow, he was killed in the first engagement a month later.

and there is plenty of it. I have noticed that our entire forces are well supplied with wholesome food—excellent beef brought from Australia, good bread, and good coffee. The men fare as well as the officers. The hospitals and their corps are also reported to be in fine condition and well managed, and have there ever been reports to the contrary?—yet, this is Manila, thousands of miles from home; almost as far as was Montauk Point!

Is, or is not, this state of affairs in Manila a criticism upon the camp at Montauk? I have been asked by several men over here why, as Montauk was "approved" as a camp site in *June*, the essentials of a camp were not at once placed there; why no move was made until one week before the hospital ships arrived in August. It certainly was known that they would come, and surely they would be ordered to a site "approved" weeks before. I have also been asked why the hotel at Fire Island—owned by the Government—was not used for the sick and dying, or why others such as that at Long Beach were not purchased. I confess that I could not answer the questions.

What may be the result upon our soldiers of a summer in these islands remains to be seen, but certainly up to this time—January 15, 1899—they all appear to be in good condition, happy, and contented.

The drive back from Manila to the city takes one past barracks after barracks, all crowded with our soldiers, apparently having a very good time. Many of the old Spanish barracks are in use, but, being insufficient, vast buildings of framework, walled with matting and heavily thatched, have been erected. They are all raised some three feet from the ground, are but one story in height, and are composed chiefly of vast, open windows. Therefore the danger from fire cannot be great, and fire-escapes are certainly not necessary. The men are at their ease, but I notice that their guns stand stacked near by, and the sentries are many and vigilant.

January 14, 1899.—There seems to be an unusual amount of subdued excitement to-night! Rumours of all sorts fill the city, and the monitor *Monadnock* is constantly sweeping the country down by Malate with her powerful search-lights. The *Monterey* has steam up, ready to join her on call. Instructions are to the soldiers to be prepared to-morrow with pick and spade to throw up earthworks if necessary, and the announcement was sent to all headquarters that the rebels would come around to church to-morrow and begin operations all over town immediately thereafter. They are allowed during the day to come and go—without arms—as they please, and our men have orders to avoid all hostilities. Yesterday, when our sentries fell back half a mile to avoid a party of insurgents, our boys were indignant and sure of treachery. It will go hard with these people when they press our men too far. They will find no cowards, as they now believe each and every American to be.

Nine P.M. brings rumours that the attack is to be made to-night. The Escolta is deserted, and foreign flags are everywhere. An English one floats over the hotel just before my window. I have no idea

NATIVE STREET, MANILA.

that the peace will be disturbed just yet, and I really think, if we can avoid a conflict and keep on the even tenor of our way, yielding nothing, and ceasing all communications or proclamations to the so-called leaders, that matters will quiet down; that trade interests will effect what no proclamation will do; that the people, finding they are dealt honestly and justly by, and have nothing to find fault with, will return to work and business; and that, the wheels of commerce once started, self-interest and the acquisition of wealth will settle the matter. As affairs stand now, these people have no standard to judge us by, save the Spanish, and they fully believe that our treatment of them will be as bad as that they have received during the last three centuries. It will be seen further along that the English merchants here do not agree with my idea in the very least.

The plot of the "Brotherhood of Human Bloodhounds" to massacre all the Americans in Manila last week, which was frustrated by the vigilance of General E. S. Otis, is now believed to have been planned by the Tagal natives. Three men were told off to finish each American officer, but, being forewarned, the danger was slight.

These human bloodhounds are the lowest order of the Tagalos. They have the keenness of scent of animals, and are bound together by a "blood brotherhood." This is a secret society known as the *Katipunan*.

The peculiar acuteness of the Tagalos' scent is so great that the appearance of the nose itself is somewhat different to that in the rest of the human race, the nostrils having such power of dilation and expansion in action that they make long-drawn lines upon the cheeks, reaching to the eye.

The Katipunan society to which they belong was organised seven or eight years before the outbreak of the rebellion against the Spanish—which began in the Philippines in 1896. It was originally formed with the intention of resisting the Spanish tax exactions and oppressive local laws.

From this it drifted into a society of immense power. It included among its members the richest and most educated of the Mestizos and also a number of native priests when it commenced its aggressive operations against the Spanish Government, and the rebellion of 1896 was inaugurated. For sixteen months the island of Luzon was devastated by a war which for ferocious cruelties on the part of the Spaniards and fearful retaliations on the part of the Filipinos has scarcely ever been equalled.

The "blood brotherhood" mark of the Katipunan is made generally on the left forearm, though sometimes on the left knee, by a curious knife covered with symbols of the society.

All who join the Katipunans sign the roll in their own blood, the third finger of the left hand being pricked at the tip until the blood runs, and with that blood they sign. Then, as a sure sign of membership, a vein is opened in the left forearm in such fashion that the wound will certainly leave a scar, or else a wound is made in the left breast that will leave a round scar like a vaccination mark.

The first great plot of the Katipunan society was to assassinate General Blanco when he was Governor of the Philippines. The date set for this was September 15, 1896, and it was planned to take advantage of the confusion following his death to slaughter all the Spaniards, and seize the citadel and the fortifications of Manila, with its batteries, arsenal, and barracks.

One press correspondent has gone to bed disgusted because of my prophecy that there will be no disturbance of the city during the night. A steady downpour of rain comes about midnight and lasts all night. I know that that has ended it for the time, and so it proves, as morning finds the town peaceful and quiet. There is nothing like an application of water for these nations. The New York Fire Department, if it could be transported here in working order and full power, would end this question in the city promptly. In fact, what fire force they have here will be most effective in case of a street disturbance.

There are two English newspapers in Manila, *The Times* and *The Announcer*. The latter came out yesterday and stated that there were four thousand Spanish prisoners over in the old town that had enlisted with the insurgents. There were several other statements not calculated to smooth matters for the Americans. J—— of *The Times* states that had that notice appeared in his paper it would have "promptly been held up by the powers that be," and that he was called to account because he termed Aguinaldo's proclamation "hysterical." What does this mean? Has the freedom of the press passed away? Why is one paper favoured and another suppressed? Surely nothing could be more inoffensive than *The Times.* I was asked yesterday if I would carry a package of dispatches to Hong Kong, as nothing of any importance was allowed to pass our censors.

Sunday has gone by with no disturbance of the city's calm. Monday brings two alarms of fire, and consequently a general call for the entire force. Even now comes another, and the Escolta is filled with rushing soldiers in blue and brown, white-clad Spaniards, dark-skinned Filipinos, slow-going bullock-carts, rapidly moving carriages, and ponies of all shapes and sizes, all getting out of the path of supposed danger. In less than half an hour the entire lot comes back laughing.

As we are about to start for a drive to our outposts, where I fancy we shall find a very wet lot of boys, judging by last night's rain, we witness a scene between a Spanish officer and a Tagalo which is strongly indicative of the feelings between the races. The officer was walking quietly along when the Tagalo suddenly spat in his face. A fight quickly ensued which brought our sentry promptly to the spot. When he fully understood the cause of the disturbance he handed his gun to the Spaniard, and, taking the latter's cane, gave the Tagalo a sound thrashing, which was not lessened in its thoroughness by our applause.

Personally I have experienced but one act of hostility from the Spaniards since my arrival. It occurred this morning as I was standing on the curb enjoying the ever-changing panorama of the Escolta. An officer in passing suddenly jabbed me in the ribs with such force as almost to throw me into the street.

I think he thought that I was one of his own race, as I am somewhat swarthy, and was dressed in white with a broad-brimmed hat; but, if so, my remarks in the American tongue and American accent promptly undeceived him, and the expression of his face changed to terror as he saw me speak to one of our sentries, to whom I related the incident, at the same time refusing, to the sentry's disgust, to point out the man. He had been punished enough, to judge from his scared face fleeing up the street before us. As we passed along I asked one man—from Dakota—if he expected to be assassinated, but he answered, "There are not enough niggers in the islands to kill us off." Perhaps not, if it were a fair, open fight.

Many ladies have taken refuge on the ships in the harbour, and if matters grow really serious many more of them will go to the fort. Colonel F—— invites me to make the move, but this hotel is safe enough, and one sees everything here on the Escolta.

CHAPTER XX

TRIBES OF THE ISLANDS—PHILIPPINE LEADERS

Origin of the Filipinos—The Negritos—The Gaddanes—The Head-Hunters—The Fire Tree—Our Men in this Climate—Spain and the Hill Tribes—The Tagalos—Their Love of Dress—Native Costume—Aguinaldo and his Associates—Their Robbery of the People—Their Condition and Desires—Their Characters—Chinese "Houses of Pleasure"—The Dishonesty of the People—The Impossibility of a Protectorate over these People—Position of the United States—Our Knowledge of the Outer World.

THE origin of the peoples of these islands is a matter of dispute. Chili, Peru, and Malaysia are all mentioned as their cradles. The Negritos are found in all parts of the archipelago. Foreman says that they are cowardly and will only attack a retreating foe, or from behind safe defences. That seems to be a characteristic of all these peoples. The Negritos are wonderfully swift runners; they are spirit-worshippers; they respect age and the dead, and in the latter characteristic are certainly the superior of the Tagalos. They possess little or no intellect. They always live in the mountains, and, like the blacks of Australia, their natural instincts force them at times to return to their old lives and pursuits, no matter how long they may

PETTY KING OF THE TINGNANOS, WITH GUARDS, LUZON.

have dwelled amidst civilised people, or how much care has been taken with their education.

The Gaddanes in the northern end of Luzon are the most ferocious tribe on the island. No attempt has been made to civilise or even subdue them. They are the head- or scalp-hunters, and a bridegroom always presents his father-in-law with all such trophies that he can capture. When the "fire tree" blooms they go on the war-path, celebrate certain rites, and it will be well to be absent at that period. With the arrow and lance they can accomplish wonders. Have we a William Penn in our land who can reach and affect these people? If we try subjugation, we shall once more pass through a period like that in our own land from 1620 to the present day, and our men cannot endure this climate as our race has done that of America throughout the long period of our struggle with the Indians. Save when on the war-path, these people are lazy and indolent.

Spain has never in any way conquered these islands, though she has possessed more power in Luzon than elsewhere. On one island, Mindanao, a sultan holds supreme authority, merely paying a small tribute to Spain. On another she has held a few coast towns, while all the interior was given over to savages — savages worshipping the sun, wood, and stone. In the northern end of Luzon, even the insurgents will not travel in parties of less than twenty, for fear of the Negritos and head-hunters, of which there are from sixty to eighty thousand. These tribes have never known anything about Spain or any other nation outside of their own race, yet they are probably as well qualified to become enfranchised Americans as are many of the immigrants that are annually landed in New York.

Had England found in the Maoris of New Zealand such a race as any of these, her story to-day would have been far different in that island, and her only hope would have been extermination. She has had no success with the blacks of Australia, who are fast dying out. Her conquest of India was over races that could scarcely be considered barbarous, and that were far from savages. We may call them heathen, but races that can produce the Taj Mahal, the mosques of Delhi and of Agra, the temples at Tanjore and Rameswaram, cannot be called even barbarous. These mountain tribes are savages like our own, and worse, and our success with our home product has not been much to be proud of. The Tagalos, who claim to be the patriots, and with whom we are at war, are but one race among many. They are about up to the average Malay races in stature, but are rather inferior as to intellect. Certainly they are not to be compared mentally to the Maoris of New Zealand.

It would seem that a love of dress is not, under all circumstances, undesirable, as, in the case of these Tagalos, the market for European goods, such as hats and shoes, is larger than in all British and Dutch East India. One's servant is often better shod and covered than one's self. He will not wear shoes of English make—they are too heavy and coarse. Those from Vienna please him better.

The costume of the men consists of a pair of trousers and a shirt, the latter being made out of a

TAGAL WOMAN, MANILA.

thin gauze material, perfectly transparent, and often embroidered. The dress of the women is more distinctly national, and is very picturesque. They wear no stockings, but thrust the bare feet into a pair of high-heel pattens with wooden soles and velvet tips. There is nothing to hold them on save these tips, yet the wearers move along swiftly and in a stately fashion. The rest of the costume seems composed of a white undergarment, low-necked and short-sleeved, a full skirt of calico or silk, sometimes with a train, be the wearer ever so youthful, over which is worn a long black silk apron, which crosses behind. The most distinctive garment, however, is the low-necked jacket which falls short of the belt, and has wide, full, but short, elbow sleeves. A white kerchief is often worn around the neck, and the hair is neatly twisted on the head. They look clean, yet from the toilet scenes which one constantly witnesses, one is forced to the conclusion that it is but an appearance.

Notwithstanding the instructions of the friars, the natives resemble the Burmese in their belief as to the wandering of a soul from a sleeping body, and hence their dislike to awaken anyone. "The soul might not return." The Tagalo feigns friendship, but has no loyalty, and is a remarkable combination of virtues and vice.

Aguinaldo is a full-blooded Tagalo of about twenty-six years of age, medium in stature, with short, thick, black hair worn pompadour. Some consider him sharp and shrewd, but it is generally believed that he has his price, though it would be a large one. It is also claimed that he is swayed in all directions by the different parties, all of which have their own schemes to work out, and any one of which will sell out the others.

They have already enriched themselves at the expense of their people, and boast thereof. Of course they cannot hope to retain these ill-gotten gains if we hold the islands. The people would give us but little trouble, but these self-styled patriots, self-appointed rulers, will be content with but one condition of affairs: First, that the American Government shall supply a chain of war-ships around the islands to keep off all outside interference. Second, that the entire management of the islands be placed in the hands of this gang of men, especially all offices that enable them to carry out the methods they have learned from three centuries of Spanish teaching. They desire particularly the power to coin money—for themselves. As is always the case, they would be more intolerant of the people, from whose ranks they have so lately risen, than were the Spaniards. What character of men they are will be more fully understood when it is known that Aguinaldo, in the proclamation of his constitution, announced that his government would "*license the Chinese houses of pleasure*." To the uninitiated this sounds innocent enough, yet through such "pleasures" came the destruction of Sodom and Gomorrah.

It would be difficult to find anyone in Manila who believes in the patriotism of these Tagalos. Money will buy the leaders at any time. As for the masses, they are lazy and dishonest; they will lie and steal to the very last. The manager of one of

AGUINALDO AND ASSOCIATES.

1. Aguinaldo.	2. Montenegro.	3. Natividad.
4. Niniegra.	5. Ziño.	6. Belarmino.
7. Covinting.	8. Mascordo.	9. Arbacho.
10. G. Pilar.	11. Niola.	12. Francisco.
13. Slansra.		

the large banks told me that he caught a boy stealing some gold and took the money from his hand, yet the fellow denied having touched it. Moral suasion was tried to induce him to tell why he had stolen it, but he again denied the theft, and, upon being flogged, remarked, " Why do you whip me for what I did not do ? " Perhaps under different training these people might to-day show different results; perhaps the training they have received is the direct cause of these results. However that may be, such are the results, and it is rather wearisome to those who have been out here, and who know the true characters of these people, to listen to the sentimental and ignorant twaddle at some of the meetings at home concerning the " struggling patriotism " which we are condemned for suppressing, and to hear these corrupt and degraded leaders compared to Kossuth.

It has been announced in our Senate that we will merely " extend a protectorate over the Philippine Islands until their people should become able to govern themselves." From our Anglo-Saxon standpoint, when will that be ? Will we consent to a continuance of the manners and customs of Old Spain, or rather to an exaggeration of those manners and customs?—for such it would be! It is easy enough to contract a bad habit, but it is quite another matter to overcome it. I fear it will be somewhat longer than three hundred years before we can consider these people " fit to govern themselves," and the same will hold true in Cuba. And Santo Domingo and Hayti must also come under our dominion. A state of barbarity exists there which would rival any to be found in darkest Africa.

If the United States had desired to give up these islands, or rather not to take them, she should have left them in Spanish hands. We cannot return them to that kingdom. We cannot surrender them to any other nation, even to England, although we might be willing to do so to her. We certainly cannot in common decency and humanity abandon them to the natives, knowing that an awful state of anarchy would ensue. As I have before stated, the so-called rulers, corrupt in every way, would promptly make cause with the worst class of the friars, who could no more be drawn off than a vulture from the "Towers of Silence." The result would be chaos.

If, however, those two powers should fail, the people would, in very short order, return to a state of barbarity, and we should have the reproach of the whole world. Whether we like it or not we have put our hand to the plough, or the handles thereof have been placed in our hands by a Higher Power, and we must perform the allotted task; and surely there are none in America willing to acknowledge that we are not capable of doing so. We must learn—but we can learn.

There are some examples to be avoided, notably that of Holland. Through selfishness, she has built a wall, so to speak, around her possessions in the East, and does not desire them to hold intercourse with the outer world save through herself. The Dutch cities of Java are beautiful to look upon, but the government is hidebound and provincial. It has changed little since the days of the famous Dutch East India Company, when it was death to trade with any save the Dutch in the four great spices. The progress of the nineteenth century has alone caused her to modify that at all. One cannot but regret that England exchanged those islands for Ceylon. She might have known that Ceylon would come to her under any circumstances, and the condition of affairs in Java and Sumatra would be far different if the English flag floated there to-day, while the world would not be in such comparative ignorance concerning them as we find it.

Our people should attempt to in some degree appreciate the work other nations are doing in the outer world, and thereby fully understand the place America must take, the work she must do, and her duty to the rest of mankind, unless she means to build a wall around herself for all time, unless she means to lead a purely selfish life, and thereby become the laughing-stock of the nations, while she lays herself open to just contempt.

CHAPTER XXI

TRADE IN THE PHILIPPINES

Siege by the British—Return to Savage Instincts—Unable to Govern Themselves—Spain's Dealing with the People—Smuggling in Money—The Mexican Dollar—English Opinion of the Islands—Mountains and Rivers—Effect of Railways—Dissatisfaction over our Tariff—English Clubs—English Advice and Opinion of the Tagalos.

THE successful siege of Manila by the British in 1762 needs no further mention. The fierce quarrels which followed their evacuation of that city would be enacted to-day if we were to surrender to the natives—quarrels which ended only after great loss of life. There seems to have been a constant succession of rebellions down to the present time. Foreman, in his most interesting book, *The Philippine Islands*, states that had these rebellions succeeded they would have produced "a state of protracted anarchy, intensified by the return of the wayward natives to their savage instincts, for they are far from being able to govern themselves on any civilised plan."

The government and local administration have cost some $350,000 per annum, of which $40,000 went to the Governor-General; but that was but a drop in the bucket that each sent away, pressed down and running over. There have been honest governors in these islands, but they have been few and far between, and their lives have not been happy. I am told by one who has lived in Manila for twelve years that in all that time he has never met a Spanish official who could speak the native tongue. These officials never remained longer than three years, and rarely so long, and made no attempt to learn the language, nor did they take any interest in the natives save to rob and debauch them.

Spain's manner of dealing with the half-castes was in marked distinction to that of Holland in the East. The latter Government, after educating this race, gave them the opportunity to utilise that education by means of the many positions and offices of the land. But not so with Spain. She established colleges and schools, gave a certain education, but there it stopped, and the half-castes and natives were not allowed to occupy any of the governmental offices. Every post and position which was worth a dollar was given only to Spaniards. Of course, this produced discontent and, in the end, rebellion.

Hard times came in Manila with the depreciation of silver. Up to that time gold had been more plentiful than the white metal. The Mexican dollar—worth about fifty cents—was introduced, and the Government, desiring to stop this, instead of declaring that it would not be a legal tender, attempted to prohibit its importation. Of course, the people at once took to smuggling the white metal. If discovered, the smuggler lost a quarter of his holdings, the other three quarters being returned to him on the ship and sent out of the country. It is unnecessary to state that the high officials who had nothing to do with the detection got the lion's share of that "quarter," while the Government got nothing, and the actual detective little more. This could end in but one way: the detection ceased, and the detectives went into the business in partnership with the ship's captain. Then the Government declared that only the coins—Mexican—prior to a certain date would be accepted as legal tender. At once an immense and profitable business in old coins began. At Hong Kong and Singapore every ship brought in a lot, and ten and fifteen per cent. was cleared in a day or so on these transactions. All of the officials joined in, and the Spanish consul at Singapore was in the habit of sending a hundred dollars over by every ship, a favour in which the captain must oblige him, or stand the chances of being injured through the papers, etc.

Through all this, poor Spain slept on and on, and if questioned put it all off to *mañana*, that fatal day for the old empire, and again slept on and on, while her children cut her throat and sucked out her life-blood.

The English here hold that these islands are of the greatest value as to trade, that they produce almost everything needful, but as yet they have scarcely been scratched, so to speak. Coal is found in great abundance, and it is supposed that the precious metals abound.

The real wealth, however, is drawn from the raw materials obtained by agriculture and forest produce.

POLITICAL EXECUTION, MANILA.

Cigars are manufactured in large quantities, but some claim that they do not stand a long voyage, and would not be fresh in America. It is also said that they are not well made. So far, sugar and hemp appear to be the greatest staples of the islands. Coffee is not produced on a very extensive scale. There is but one crop a year, while in the West Indies the berry may be gathered during eight months of the year. Tobacco was brought here from Mexico in the earliest days by the priests. It has been a Government monopoly in the island of Luzon, but does not appear to have been so in the other islands of the archipelago.

The climate of Luzon is only semi-tropical, as the foliage testifies. In the neighbourhood of Manila there are mountains of eight thousand feet in altitude, upon which all climates may be found, and there delightful houses and sanitariums could be built. The island of Luzon has one river of great size—the Rio Grande, which flows from the south to the north, and must be at least two hundred miles in length. The volume of water is very great.

In the Philippines the building of those great civilisers, the railways, should be pushed to the utmost. Their construction will, more than anything else, tend to open up the country and settle the disputed points, and in their construction we can use Chinese labour. It is the general opinion among business men in Manila that we would be wise to do so. There are plenty of that race now here, and they can endure the climate and will work, whereas labourers from our country cannot endure the climate, and the natives will not work. The

English merchants in Manila are becoming very dissatisfied with the present condition of trade. They claim that it is much worse than when the Spaniards had control, for then the wheels did move, though bribery was often necessary. Still the amounts demanded were nothing when compared with the duties exacted by our laws, and which have completely paralysed all business, and will, they claim, if continued, end in the undoing of Manila.

At present the American Government holds only this city, which does not represent Luzon by a large majority. All of the rest of the island is in the hands of the insurgents, who carry out the old Spanish customs. Naturally this will end in business seeking those outlets and inlets. It is interesting to listen to the conversation at the Tiffin Club and the English Club, which are frequented by all the bankers and business men of the city. I asked one of them what England would have done if in our place.

"Taken all the ports at least, and at once, for only thereby can you control the trade. The conquest of the rest of the islands could be left to time. But your idea that the return of business prosperity, and a possible increase of money to the nation, would, in any way, influence these Tagalos, is not correct. They are too idle and lazy, and care absolutely nothing about money, or the things money can buy. A poor man in England will have some few household goods, which will force him to have an abiding-place, but these people own nothing, absolutely nothing, save a change of clothing, and not always or often that much. Their houses are devoid of all furniture; they sleep on mats, which being rolled around their clothes can be carried on a man's head, and the family is ready to move. Where to, is a matter which concerns them not at all. Any shelter will answer. As for food, they live on rice, bananas, and dried fish; the first two items cost nothing at all, and the last a mere song. They have no ambition, they beat their women, and offer their daughters to any white man for a small sum. Indeed such a relation is considered an honour to the girl, especially if it results in a child which will be whiter than herself. Their only redeeming trait is a faithfulness after marriage, and short shrift would the woman or her lover receive if discovered. Their knives are long and sharp."

I had to confess that we knew nothing at all about colonisation, and was promptly asked why then we did not ask England to help us—that was a thing "she could do, and was very willing to do. She has a large colonial force of clerks, etc., also higher officers, who understand this work through years of experience. She has native soldiers, from her colonies, accustomed to these climates, and policemen in the habit of dealing with Asiatics. She could carry on the whole matter for a few years, or until the United States was ready for the work, when she would hand back the islands for your guidance. The resources of the Philippines are enormous, yet not even a fraction thereof has been developed. The English know all this, and your people should know it, but it is terrible for us to have business interests choked and at a standstill, and this will continue as long as your tariff is applied here."

It is very evident that England would be delighted to obtain possession of these islands, and no doubt would gladly exchange her West Indies for them. Those islands would, of course, be infinitely less care to us, but, from a trade standpoint, are not to be compared to the Philippines. If we make the trade, let us do so with full comprehension.

CHAPTER XXII

CAVITE

Impossible to Travel through the Islands—Courtesy of Admiral Dewey—His Appearance and Character—Manila Bay—Our Fleet—The Spanish Ships—Cavite—Fortress and Arsenal—Its Appearance—Desecrated Churches—Ruined Alameda—Forts of the Town—End of the Spanish Empire—The Pageant of Centuries—Spain's Present Condition and Opportunities—Departure on the *Zafiro*—Island of Corregidor—The Southern Cross—Spanish Prizes—Hong Kong—Affected by the War—China the Coming Country—Old Shanghai and its Horrors.

IT is with great regret that I leave Manila without having travelled through the islands, but in the present state of unrest it is not possible. Our own authorities can offer no protection and do not want travellers to go, and I cannot but appreciate their reasons, and bow to their decision. If known as an American, I should probably be imprisoned or killed, all of which would make trouble. It might be possible to go if I were willing to pass as an Englishman, but pride alone would prevent an American in Manila from sailing under any colours save his own.

It is certainly the proper thing to say farewell to the city from the midst of Admiral Dewey's fleet. Thanks to the courtesy of the Admiral, I am leaving on the Government ship *Zafiro*, which is used as a dispatch-boat between here and Hong Kong, and have been requested to be at the custom-house dock at 11 A.M., in order to be taken on board. As I pass to the wharf, the launch of the Admiral steams up and he comes out of the door just behind me.

Admiral Dewey seems to possess the quality which made the first Napoleon great, *i. e.*, the ability to move while his enemies are yet thinking. He is a much better-looking man than his portraits would lead one to expect. His face is delicate and refined, but full of strength. His dark eyes express great determination, and his firm chin carries out the expression. I was strongly reminded as I looked at him of those words in Whittier's *Snow-Bound*: "A prompt, decisive man, no breath our father wasted: 'Boys, a path!'" I for one cannot but think, with all due consideration for the present Governor of Manila, that if Admiral Dewey had been appointed to that post, there would long since have been made "a path" to that goal from which we seem afar off just now. The Admiral, however, is one of the President's new board in these islands, and his influence will undoubtedly be strongly felt.

We did not see the great bay of Manila on our way in, as we arrived at early dawn; but leaving now at 11 A.M., we have full sight of it on the way out, and a beautiful vision it is with its shores sweeping north and south in magnificent circles, its waters sparkling under a brilliant sun. The bay is as large as Port Philip in Australia, and the scenery is far more beautiful, as it is bordered by mountains from four to seven thousand five hundred feet in height, Mount Ararat to the north being somewhat higher than our Mount Washington.

As to exact size, the surveys show the bay to be some forty miles from north to south, and twenty-seven from Manila to the island of Corregidor, which blocks its entrance; and save for the channels on either side of this island, it is completely land-locked, and would furnish refuge for all the shipping of the world.

The old city glows with a rosy light as our ship steams westward. Behind the country is green and beautiful, and far inland the mountains rise a dark blue mass against a darker sky.

Cavite is reached either in a small tug or in the Government launch, but it is more interesting to go in the latter, as it carries the mails to all of the fleet. The bay is full of transports—but no flag is to be seen save our own, except on the Spanish steamers, where the red and yellow looks very lonely. We first reach our man-of-war *Concord*, then the flagship *Olympia*, then the *Charleston* and the *Boston*, and, finally, the two monitors *Monterey* and *Monadnock;* all have steam up, all are painted grey and are very warlike in appearance. Yonder are several merchantmen at anchor, and one full-rigged ship, the *Vigilant* of Boston. There are, also, several Spanish men-o'-war, all out of commission just at present, and likely to remain so. There could have been very little water beneath their keels when they sank, as even now boats on their davits would not touch the surface line. Four wrecks lie near Cavite Point, and one or two farther out. Three ships have been raised and are now at Hong Kong, and two more are here.

The fortress, arsenal, and town of Cavite are on an island, connected by a causeway with the mainland; but to-day, on account of threatened troubles, no one is allowed to pass beyond the causeway.

Our officers say that for several days the natives have been leaving this town, and Manila as well. Looking backward towards that city, we see that the whole valley behind it is clouded with the smoke of many fires. What it means no one can yet tell, but all the troops and war-ships are under orders to be prepared to act at a moment's notice.

On approaching Cavite, a small fort is noticed on its extreme point, with the muzzles of several cannon projecting over the top, and several more can be discovered turned topsy-turvy. This enclosure is a small one, with antiquated walls, and it could not have made any great show of resistance. Back of the arsenal are the workshops, officers' quarters, and parade-ground, while along the open sea to the right stretch the long line of the defences.

But first we visit the old city, leaving the forts for our return trip. It is a melancholy, out-of-the-way sort of a place, which, since the destruction by the insurgents, presents a scene of utter desolation. The long narrow streets, bordered by the usual two-storied houses, stretch away, empty and deserted, save by our soldiers and a handful of natives, to the public squares. American voices and language furnish the only sounds of life which greet our ears. A church on the public square stands rifled and desecrated, and of the five sacred edifices of the town, all save one are in the same condition; that one is still used for sacred purposes. Near the Alameda stands the cathedral, outwardly as it has stood for three centuries, but within it is empty and wretched. The altar is destroyed, the cloisters are a mass of ruins, and with the exception of some general who still rests, as he has rested for two hundred and fifty years, under his marble slab before the eastern portal of the church, even the graves have been dug up and their contents thrown to the winds of heaven. All this destruction was wrought by the insurgents.

Throughout the ruins of this once crowded place of rest and prayer we are the only living things, and the echo of our footsteps takes on an almost sobbing tone as they die away into silence. Passing into the Alameda, which stretches by the sea, desolation again prevails. Trees are torn and broken as though a tempest had passed by, the band-stand is a ruin, the houses are closed and in decay, and a marble statue, " a Cristobal Colon," erected only a few years since, stands headless and tottering to its fall.

From the Alameda toward the Point extend the main fortifications. They are constructed of a porous stone into which the cannon-balls sink like water into a sponge, shattering little or not at all. Every here and there are bastions where cannon should have been put, but were not. On the inner side are the barracks and storehouses, and at one end is a somewhat more pretentious bit of fortification, but it has no strength to withstand modern ordnance, and it would appear that in so far as the immediate fortifications of the town are concerned, the destruction by time has been much greater than by the guns of our fleet. At least, it is difficult to discern which is which.

Looking seaward, the Spanish flag-ship, sunken and wrecked, is the first object which strikes the eye. One funnel still stands erect, the other is half overturned, the destruction of the craft being so complete that it would be useless to attempt to raise and repair it. Here and there are the other Spanish ships in like condition, and off beyond them rides our fleet, presenting an entirely uninjured appearance, a gigantic appearance when compared to the greatest of those of Spain. I really believe that the *Olympia*, alone and unaided, could have performed the entire task of destruction.

So the end has come—the sunken wrecks here at Cavite and outside of Santiago mark the close of the ancient power of Spain. The mind must be dead indeed that will not travel backward into the past as it contemplates the scenes of all this undoing. How the panorama of the past unrolls itself as one gazes on the placid waters of Manila Bay, where rests this portion of the last of the empire's fleets! The pageant of the centuries moving across one's mental vision causes one's thoughts, travelling eastward, to pause an instant at the name of Pizarro, and the conquest of the Incas and South America; causes the mind to linger in the City of Mexico, calling up the sights that Cortez witnessed—the high "teocalli" with their human sacrifices, Montezuma and his fantastic pageants, all swept away in the waves of blood which followed the advent of the

CAVITE BAY AND ARSENAL, SHOWING SPANISH WRECKS.

Cross of Christ. Eastward yet, one's fancy wanders to Cuba and that fair circle of isles of the sea that saw Spain's first adventurers to those western lands, eastward again until the vast empire of Charles V. stands forth on the pages of history. Then Spain ruled the world. But even then the tide had turned—even then the Inquisition, by its utter disregard of all the rights of men, had signed her death-warrant.

The brilliant reign of Charles V. was the culmination of Spain's glory and power. After his death came the long struggle with the "Low Countries" and their final independence, which left Spain financially exhausted and shorn of some of her richest possessions. The expulsion of the Moors in 1610, which drove half a million of her best craftsmen with their arts and industries from the land, was another serious blow to her prosperity. If Spain had had enlightened and progressive rulers, her future would have been far different; but fate willed it otherwise. The disciples of Torquemada ruined the land itself, Drake swept the great Armada from the ocean. Philip died broken-hearted in the gloomy Escorial, tortured by remorse for the young Don Carlos and the beautiful Elizabeth of France—died by a death more horrible than any invented by his Inquisition; and thereafter the kingdom lost more and more of her splendour and of her colonies.

As the years passed on, all in North and South America and Mexico were lost to her, and all of the islands of the seas save Cuba, Porto Rico, and these Philippines, and now the youngest nation on earth has taken those from her, and her day is done. The corruption of centuries has met its just reward. The panorama has rolled away, the curtain has fallen forever on the ancient empire; if, however, there is any honesty of purpose, any desire for enlightenment and progress, her rulers may yet make a nation out of what is left. But they must change her record. It must no longer show that eleven millions out of eighteen millions of her own home people cannot read or write. All the world wishes her well, but she must awaken to the fact that this is the nineteenth century, and that the Dark Ages, with their manners and customs, their tortures, oppression, and bloodshed, are gone forever. The waters of the bay breaking around the wrecks and on the beach beneath this old fortress seem to murmur, " Forever, forever." The brilliant Stars and Stripes on yonder *Olympia*, and the bright red banner on the English man-o'-war, proclaim in louder tones, " Forever and forever."

Is it possible that a sight of their lurid banner can raise in the breasts of the Spaniards any such feeling as the people of England or America experience when they greet their flags? Can they in any degree appreciate the German word " Fatherland " ? The crimson and gold of their national emblem has meant to the masses the sacrifice of millions of their brethren in foreign wars, meant the power of the classes to oppress the people, meant the utter absence of all right or justice to the latter—therefore, how can they love it as we do ours?

A wild shriek from the *Zafiro's* whistle warns us that we must get on board. Ships and men move with promptness in the Philippines nowadays. Our ship's anchor is hoisted and we are under way before we can mount the companionway, and she does not pause even to salute the *Olympia*, though the Admiral is plainly visible on the quarter-deck. The waters are as placid as a mirror, reflecting each vessel and wreck and launch; even the flags are perfectly repeated until the waves produced by our craft turn the phantom banners into a blurred mass. Manila glows with a rosy light at the foot of her encircling mountains, while to the westward rise the dark masses of Corregidor, under whose cliffs we pass as we make for open sea.

This island of Corregidor will in time be the great pleasure and seaside resort of Manila. The top of its lighthouse rises six hundred and thirty feet above the sea, and when Manila is sweltering Corregidor is always cool and delightful.

Back in the seventeenth century a girl of seventeen years, who had taken the veil in the Santa Clara Convent, responded to the love-making of a Franciscan monk. An elopement followed, which of course created great scandal. They were pursued and finally found in a sad condition on Camaya. The friar had been nearly killed in his attempts to protect the maiden from the natives, who admired her as much as he did, and considered him selfish. They were captured by an alderman and his staff who had pursued them from Manila, the friar being sent off to teach morality to the Visaya tribes, the maiden to perpetual imprisonment in some convent in Mexico; and one cannot but wonder whether that poor body once immured in the walls of the convent of Santo Domingo, and now to be seen in the National Museum in that city, was not this romantic and unfortunate maiden. This elopement gave the name to *Corregidor* (alderman) and the rocks to the right and left of it, *Fraile* (friar) and *Monja* (nun), while the refuge is called after the girl—*Marivelas*.

With one last glance towards the lights of Corregidor, we turn away from Manila, but even as we do so, the clouds separate above the harbour, and the gleaming constellation of the Southern Cross sails high in the heavens, a constellation usually as coy as a beautiful maiden, and not often revealed in its full glory, but when it does stand forth with its attendant pointers upon the deep, dark background of the southern sky, it is magnificent, and in such guise we leave it on guard over these new possessions of ours—leave it with the hope that it may bring them greater peace than the Christian Cross has done; but the Christian Cross yet abides and is served by other disciples.

Two naval officers are the only other passengers on this ship. There is no cargo, and before we turn in, the restless China Sea has seized upon the craft and commenced to toss it to and fro. For three days it reels onward like a drunken man, and our state the while is not a happy one; but all things have an ending, and Sunday finds us in Hong Kong just in season to board the English mail for the north. I am taken ashore in a launch whose owner declines any payment because "your people have left so much money here as it is."

I have but a few hours to spare here before the *Ballaarat* sails for Shanghai, and employ the time in a visit to the Spanish ships which we have raised and sent over for repairs—the *Isla de Cuba*, *Isla de Luzon*, and the *Don Juan de Austria*. It is said that one hundred thousand dollars will put these ships in good order and make them very serviceable, but they are sorry-looking sights now, and, to the uninitiated, appear scarcely worth the trouble and expense. Six months at the bottom of the sea (they were burned by the Spaniards) has reduced them to a mass of rusty metal thickly covered with barnacles. That they could cross the tempestuous China Sea under their own steam is a marvel, and speaks much for their construction and worth.

Hong Kong is an evidence that this section of the world is on a forward march of great importance. In the nine years which have elapsed since I was here last the city has improved most markedly. Whole sections have been reclaimed from the bay, and now stand covered with blocks of stately buildings, and her business is vastly greater, and still on the increase. That affair in Manila has left millions of dollars here, and a real opening up of those islands means millions more.

China is the objective point in the business world at present, and Shanghai, so it is prophesied, will be the London of Asia. The new railway syndicates are centred there, and with the awakening of that nation a change will come over this part of the world. Mr. L. H., who has the mining rights in Corea, asserts that within three years steamships will be running directly between Shanghai and San Francisco, "leaving Japan entirely out in the cold." China is the coming country for business.

Go there if you would make a fortune—and yet what a people they are! How one dreads their advance as one would that of a pestilence! Under foreign influence they can become a clean and attractive nation—witness the Chinese section of European Shanghai, where are to be found clean streets and houses, gay signs and much gilding, sweet-scented tea-houses and concert-halls, and clean working people.

But let us leave all this brilliancy. Pass beyond the French concession to where old Shanghai stands in all its hoary antiquity. You will be deposited by your rickshaw boy at one of its many gates, will pause a moment to gaze at its grimy embattlemented wall, and then, gathering your clothing well up and around you, you will enter the city under an archway dripping with foul ooze and slime, and over a moat whose vileness cannot be described.

Nothing save a sedan-chair can pass through these narrow streets, so narrow that when two chairs meet one must be taken into a shop. We journey for hours on foot, and shall go away, if not wiser, certainly very much sadder.

Here we see the people of this ancient race dwelling as they have dwelt for centuries. The little shops are dingy but interesting, and the shopmen seem of a kindly disposition. This is the sunny side of old Shanghai, but at any moment, and it would seem at all moments, one is likely to meet with such sights and sounds of woe and horror that instant flight to where such things are not becomes necessary.

Yonder, for instance, down in the black ooze and

slime of that dark and dismal corner, is a human being such as we are—a man in full prime, who moans and sobs and beats his head into the mud and against the stones. It is bitterly cold, and his clothing is thin and ragged, and where parts of it are dragged away from his limbs he is seen to be alive with black small-pox. There is a God somewhere who may know why such things are necessary, but He does not tell us.

Let us drop the curtain on old Shanghai.

CHAPTER XXIII

LOOKING BACKWARD

Present State of Japan—Effect of the Chinese War—Fear of the Foreign Residents—Eastern Races *versus* the American Negro—Scene in Florida—Japanese Application of Western Civilisation—Their Steamships—The Chinese Prisoners—Fair Play Unknown—Filipinos Compared to Japanese.

JAPAN stands to-day at the portals of a new life. During the coming summer she will be acknowledged by the great nations as an equal, and will enter upon a most critical period in her national existence. How will she handle herself? Will she select the road to comparative peace, or will she imitate her powerful neighbour—Russia?

No nation holds more friendly feelings towards the "land of the morning" and its people than America, and much that I shall note is in direct opposition to the *generally* accepted ideas of our people concerning that nation, but travellers in those islands to-day will generally agree with what I shall state. They will each and all of them express their doubts—grave doubts—as to the outcome of the near future. Passing along, one must note many things which will not produce a favourable impression. The treatment of the people by the police savours more of the absolute unreasoning power of Russia than of that to which Americans are accustomed from those servants of the law in their own land. Those of my readers who have visited Russia will understand how much this portends. As for the people, if a man is so unfortunate as to come into actual conflict with any of them, their manner of attack will confirm his opinion that the race is far from civilised.

One is struck with the idea that Japan is in a comatose state just now. Yokohama has not improved at all in ten years, and the English and Americans look forward with growing forebodings to July next, when that city will pass under Japanese rule, the very prospect of which, they say, has blighted all the treaty ports. It is not believed that the war with China will benefit Japan in the end. It has made her people most ridiculously conceited—they are firmly convinced that they know everything and can learn nothing further, entirely forgetting that "if we do not advance, we must decline—we starve in the possessed." I am told that foreigners who can sell their property in the islands are fast doing so. They are each and all very emphatic in their denunciation of the Japanese character. "Neither his word nor his bond is of any value, whereas, once a Chinaman gives his word, it is as good as his bond—both are good." As to the honesty of the Chinese race at large,—I do not include those in official life,—the fact that they are employed in great numbers in the banks and other places where money is about speaks loudly in their favour, but one never sees a Japanese in such institutions even in Japan.

Will these Eastern nations ever accept civilisation as our Southern negroes have done? Will their lower ranks take any save an apathetic part therein? The classes have done so in Japan, but have the masses? It does not strike me that they have.

Sitting one day with my sister upon the veranda of her house in Florida, our attention was attracted by a comely young black woman who had stopped in the avenue at the side of the place. She was neatly dressed in a black gown, and wore a small black bonnet on her nicely combed hair. Taking a prayer-book and hymnal from her pocket, she bowed, and opening the former read a few verses and then offered a prayer. A chapter from the Bible was followed by a hymn, she reading a line and then singing it, until she found we would join in, when the reading was dropped and the hymn was sung to a close. Then followed a short but excellent discourse on "Love God above all, and thy neighbour as thyself," which was followed by another hymn and a benediction. Our contributions were refused, while she thanked us for the honour we had done her by our attention, and expressed the hope that she might be allowed to come again. She moved away in the sunshine and under the bending boughs of the blossoming orange trees, while we felt that our service had been quite equal to any offered to Almighty God that day in the stately churches of Christendom. How long will it be before any such scene will occur amongst these Eastern nations?

Foreign residents report the outlook in Japan as

gloomy. In most countries a man is deemed innocent until proven guilty, but they say that in Japan the reverse holds.

If the following incident is true the Japanese must lack common sense. It was related to me by the officers of the O. & O. S.S. *Gaelic*. When the Japanese new trans-Pacific ships for San Francisco first came to Yokohama they were provided with a complete staff of English officers, men who had certificates from "Lloyd's," which is the highest authority of this kind in the world, yet these men were required to go to Tokio and pass examinations before the Japanese courts. Some did so, but others refused. They could not be discharged, as they were engaged for three years; this, however, did not deter the Japs from placing another staff—of Japs—on each ship, so that to-day there are two full staffs of officers. One would imagine that this would insure good management, prompt obedience—nothing of the sort. During one of the late voyages the cargo shifted on one of the vessels and the Jap crew were ordered to replace it, but "*declined to work on the* [CHRISTIAN] *Sabbath*," and only consented to do so after extra payment was offered. It is needless to add that they were not of our faith and held no respect for it.

Those in authority in the land are utterly arbitrary and senseless in their application of things taught them by the enlightened nations. For instance, I am told of two Chinese who were lately on a Japanese steamship going from Seattle to Hong Kong. The ship stopped a day in Yokohama, but the Chinamen did not go ashore. A Japanese official, coming on board, discovered an opium pipe in the possession of one of the men, whereupon he turned them over to the police. They were taken ashore and condemned to twelve months of hard labour.

Discretion, judgment, and fair play seem unknown to the race. As their conceit has increased their art has decreased in merit in like proportion. True, there are still beautiful objects for sale, but they are few and far between, and cost more than they would bring in New York—a state of affairs very different from that which I encountered in 1890. They are a people of a different race and certainly of a much higher degree of civilisation than the Filipinos, but if such a state of affairs exists with them, what, think you, would take place in Luzon if we gave the island over to the Tagals? Truly the last state thereof would be worse than the first, for if our yoke is shaken off, civilisation will die out. The people must be guided and watched over, while the quiet influences of just laws, good schools, and pure teaching of religion are allowed to exert their power, effecting such a change as the missionaries accomplished with the Hawaiians; but the task will prove more difficult, for we must undo the terrible work of the last three centuries, must give them religious teachers—Catholic and Protestant—free from scandal, instructors whom they can respect,—then in another century, if we are true to this trust which has been thrust upon us, the world will read a far different story of the Philippine Islands.

INDEX